Advance Praise

Hillary Marotta is a wonderful writer, and I say this because reading a how-to book on nonprofits could be a bit dull, but dull it is not. It is inspiring and helpful and a great read. Serving on two nonprofit boards, I would not only recommend this book, I would say that Head and Heart *is an imperative read for all folks who run or want to run nonprofits with compassion and passion, love, and kindness. Donald Papson's foreword says it all in the first line: "This book is partially how to, partially when to, and mostly have to." Brava, Hillary, brava. You wrote a "have-to" book.*

—Amy Ferris
Author of *Marrying George Clooney: Confessions from a Midlife Crisis*

In Head and Heart, *Hillary Marotta shares practical, real-world insight and advice for nonprofit startup leaders seeking to make a sustainable difference for their cause and to stay sane doing it. In marrying common-sense business acumen with mission-driven passion, Marotta's guidance empowers nonprofit leaders to balance the "why" and the "how" of effective difference-making. From mastering the nitty-gritty details to compassionately engaging people,* Head and Heart *is a guide to increase efficiency, reduce burnout and frustration, and promote positive outcomes for the causes we care about.*

—Lisa Wade
Author of *Real. Big. Love. A Difference Maker's Guide to Gain Greater Clarity, Energy, and Impact for Your Cause and Life*

Soul, passion, and a good measure of idealism are foundational to any successful non-profit organization. But in that fiercely competitive universe, good intentions are never enough. They must be married to a realistic and clear-eyed business model, one that includes strategies for essentials like recruiting and retaining paid staff, handling volunteers, networking, fundraising, down to coming up with an appropriate office dress code.

Hillary Marotta is uniquely suited to helping others negotiate these complex and seemingly competing realities. She is a certainly a person of great heart herself. She also approaches nonprofits with a clear-eyed brilliance and insight, partially inherited from her grandfather, the former CEO of Hershey Foods, and from 20 years of her own ups and downs in the nonprofit world.

It doesn't hurt that she's a writer of wit, elegance, and generosity, always encouraging her readers to be mindful of the business stuff without ever losing the soul of the nonprofit mission. Head and Heart *is essential reading for those who yearn to make a difference.*

    —Tim Madigan
        Author of I'm Proud of You:
        My Friendship with Fred Rogers"

Head and Heart

Head and Heart

How to Run
a *Smart* and Compassionate
Nonprofit

BY HILLARY B. MAROTTA

UN-SETTLING BOOKS
Boulder, Colorado USA

Cover Design and Typography: Sally Wright Day
Editing: Maggie McReynolds
Author's photo courtesy of Tami Wagoner

ISBN: 978-1-7341645-0-3

To Carol, my 2/26

*This is partially for you, a way to carry on
your legacy after all the work we did together.
You were a writer, you helped me realize that
I am a writer, and it was not coincidence
but divine intervention
that brought us together.*

To Grandpa

*You were and will always be my hero,
not only as a businessman but also as
one of the best human beings I've ever known.
This is my bridge between your world and mine,
as I've learned we're much more alike than different.
Miss you more than you'll ever know.
All my love.*

Contents

Foreword

This book is partially how to, partially when to, and mostly have to. Hillary understands that a nonprofit organization is not only about the cause but must also be balanced with solid business practices and a focus on people. Her commentary on structure, alignment, and focus lead to great insights that can help guide stakeholders at every level, from volunteers to leadership.

I am proud to lead The M.S. Hershey Foundation, a diverse nonprofit with a single focus on cultural and educational enrichment, as set forth in 1935 by our founder, Milton S. Hershey. Hillary's grandfather, Richard Zimmerman, was the former CEO of The Hershey Company. He was a remarkable man who believed in philanthropy, both personally and through the generosity of the company he led.

It is clear that Hillary's thoughtful inspiration for writing this book is personal. She has a deep connection, through her grandfather, to one of the greatest philanthropists of the 20th century, Milton S. Hershey.

"This book is a must-read for anyone committed to creating or strengthening a successful nonprofit in today's ever-changing business climate.

Donald C. Papson
President and Executive Director
The M.S. Hershey Foundation

Introduction

Over the past 20 years, I have seen the good, the bad, and the oh-so ugly of the nonprofit world. I've worked for nonprofits that were constantly scraping by on office supplies and technology that was mid-20th century at best. I've seen established organizations that worked like well-oiled machines, always adapting to their changing communities' needs and successfully obtaining project grants and funding left and right. I've also seen more than one startup nonprofit flounder while trying to find its way, perilously on the edge of collapse at any moment. What these different organizations have all had in common is great people with big hearts, the best of intentions, and unending passion for their missions.

The successful ones have also had something else—they've had business-minded people who made smart decisions in every area including administration, finances, programs, and most importantly, people. They see themselves as nonprofit professionals and their organizations as legitimate businesses, and they are constantly strategizing the best ways to position themselves to make money to fund their missions. They know that even though they work in the "non" profit sector, they must still focus on bringing in revenue so that they can do their good work. And they know when and how to invest in the right people.

How does this help you? Since you picked up this book, I know that you already have a passion, a desire to make a difference, a yearning to serve others. I'm guessing that you already help your community in one way or another. It's a safe bet that you're hoping to make an even bigger impact by starting a nonprofit, if you haven't already.

What's cool is that you already have that passion, that innate desire to make something better, and that's awesome because I can't teach you that. But I can teach you the other things. I can show you the process by which you can decide whether or not starting a nonprofit is right for you. I can tell you what steps to follow to create a legal organization.

I can even share my crazy stories of struggle and success, pointing out the common pitfalls to avoid along the way. Most importantly, I can help you understand why running a nonprofit is as much like running a business as any for-profit company is, an idea that will put you on the path to success instead of failure. Together, we'll learn how to use both your head and your heart to build a smart, compassionate, successful nonprofit.

Throughout this book, I'll walk you through steps from the conception of an idea, through developing a legal organization, and all the way to finding the right people and avoiding common mistakes. I will cite real-world examples, often my own, of excellent processes and questionable business decisions. I will give you specific takeaways and action steps to develop the best organization you possibly can so that you can take that passion and make a bigger difference in the world.

Let's dive in.

CHAPTER 1

The Aha! Moment

*"People will forget what you said, people will
forget what you did, but people will never forget
how you made them feel.*

— MAYA ANGELOU

I t was *so hot.* My scrubs and t-shirt were slick with sweat, and the work boots, bandana, and hat I wore to protect me from mosquitos did little to keep out the grit and grime. Later, I would find dirt and dust collected in crevices I didn't even know I had.

We were seeing patients and building a new medical clinic for a community on the outskirts of Managua, Nicaragua, and we'd just finished attending a celebration for the local children who were getting ready to go back to school. I went outside and saw a bunch of boys, probably under 10 years old, in soccer jerseys, so I started to talk with them in Spanish. I asked them if they liked to play soccer, and their collective response was, "Si, pero no tenemos pelotas." Yes, they said, but we don't have soccer balls.

Boom. That was the moment. I knew, then, that my life was going to be dedicated to making a difference. The idea of being so poor that there was no money for soccer balls was beyond my comprehension. It seemed like something so simple, and yet it was out of reach for those boys. I didn't want it to be that way.

At the time, I was a junior in college who'd taken a chance on a service-learning trip to Nicaragua over spring break. I hadn't settled on a career, and I didn't know what shape "making a difference" would take. All I knew for sure was that I had never seen or experienced poverty like that. This wasn't something I could hold at a distance, like a passage from a textbook or a photograph. This was reality, and even though I was only dropping in on this reality for a week and promptly returning to my cushy, first-world lifestyle, it made enough of an impact on me that I knew I had to find a way to help.

I bet you've had that moment. That aha, that bolt of lightning, that sudden moment of clarity. Maybe you took a trip, like I did, or volunteered in a soup kitchen or library or homeless shelter, and felt your work there wasn't finished. Maybe you experienced a struggle, a health crisis, a tragedy, or a family situation that led you to become fiercely loyal to educating others on a topic that makes you emotional. Maybe you simply love animals or feel a calling to help those affected by poverty, racism, sexism, or domestic violence.

Whatever that issue is that gnaws at your heart, rumbles in your gut, or calls to you repeatedly in your dreams, you know what it is. And now you're listening more carefully to it, allowing it to nudge you to figure out how to make a bigger impact. Like me, back in Nicaragua, you may be thinking,

"How am I possibly going to make a difference? Where do I start? What do I even know about running a nonprofit?"

Whether you've had one moment of clarity or decades of experience, you're here because you're looking at launching your own nonprofit. Starting your own organization dedicated to your passion is a great way for you to make a bigger impact. It's exciting—and daunting. You can be psyched for your cause and, at the same time, completely overwhelmed. You might be overwhelmed by how to do it at all, or you might be overwhelmed by the prospect of doing it well. After all, we've all come into contact with poorly run, unprofessional nonprofits that come across more as hobbies than businesses, and they suffer as a result. They lack funds, employees and volunteers, and general direction. And that is not a good way to make a bigger impact.

But where's the money going to come from? Who's going to help? How can you make enough money to sustain the organization? And, oh my gosh, the paperwork. What about the paperwork?

Here's the good news. You already have the passion. You have the cause you want to serve and the heart for that service. No one can give you that—that comes solely from within. That enthusiasm, dedication, and devotion you have to making a difference is completely innate.

But what about all of the other stuff? Those millions of questions about the day-to-day, the formation, and the success of a nonprofit? The head for business? Here's where this book comes in. Those things might not be the sexy topics or the tasks you dream about when you envision running your own organization, and they may worry you. Totally valid.

This is no small task, for sure. It will take time and patience, and certainly money. But thankfully, there are specific steps to follow and ways to break down every task into more manageable pieces. There are always people willing to invest and hands willing to help if you look in the right places.

The best news of all is that it's your organization. That means you get to define your own success and work toward it in a way that is sustainable for you. Should you choose to run a small side business because you have to maintain your full-time job, you can do that. If you want to pour your heart and soul into building an organization that could grow into something national or international, you can do that too. Your organization will be what you want it to be, in the way that you want it to be. In addition, if you set up your organization smartly and properly, and avoid some common pitfalls, you won't have to reinvent the wheel. You can build on others' good ideas to create and run an organization that is both smart and compassionate. This book will help you do just that.

One of the best things that came out of my trips to Nicaragua was the lasting relationship I formed with one of those little boys in the soccer uniforms. His name was Enyuel, and he was 11 years old. Several times, over the course of the week I was there translating in the medical clinic and mixing cement by hand, Enyuel would appear and hang out with me, standing just slightly shorter than me even though I was 10 years his senior. We'd talk a bit about his family, school, and what he wanted to be when he grew up. We took some pictures together at the end of the week so we'd remember each other—as if I could ever forget him. I had no idea if we'd ever see each other again, which made me feel both tremendously grateful we met and terribly sad.

But the story didn't end there. The following year, when I returned to Nicaragua, we were in the midst of finishing and dedicating a brand-new medical clinic we had helped to fund and build. There was a special dedication ceremony at which I had the honor of speaking on behalf of our university. There was dancing and singing, beautiful costumes and decorations. The community members who had helped every inch of the way showed such pride in their work. It was a wonderful, very emotional celebration. When it concluded, I had to step away from the crowd so I could do the ugly cry alone.

I stood bawling and looking at the new clinic that would serve thousands. It was modest—a concrete building with a few different rooms, all with grey cement walls and white tile. It had a very simple bathroom, pharmacy, and waiting area with actual chairs, luxuries by Nicaraguan standards. The community had landscaped it with small trees and flowering shrubs that would grow to provide much-needed shade later on. In comparison to a new medical clinic in the U.S., it was nothing, but in Nueva Vida, the Nicaraguan neighborhood to some 15,000 people, it was a godsend. I was admiring the building, and the dedication and hard work that brought it there, when there was a tap on my shoulder. I turned, and there was Enyuel. I couldn't believe my eyes! We shared a huge hug, which made me cry even harder. Although I had snail-mailed him the photo of us once it was developed (it was the year 2000, after all), I had no way of knowing whether he had received it or even remembered me. There was also no telling if I would ever return, and if I did, when. Yet he came back and checked for me. Then he did something even more surprising—he reached in his pocket and pulled out the photo of us together from the previous year. I was incredulous. He didn't know if I'd ever return, yet he carried our picture in his pocket for a year just in case.

******

Though I haven't been back to Nicaragua, I think of Enyuel often, hoping and praying that he was able to go to school, find work, and help take care of his mom, as his dad had died in a hurricane when Enyuel was young. A little piece of my heart will always be there with him. Those trips are what planted the seed for me to start a twenty-year career in the nonprofit sector. Those twenty years taught me what to do and what not to do when starting and running a nonprofit, and it's this hard-won wisdom I want to share with you. I've seen the good, the bad, and the ugly with small and midsize nonprofits of all kinds. I want to help you build a successful nonprofit organization to expand your impact on others, reach a wider number of people, and make a greater difference in people's lives. It will be a challenging adventure. But it will also be exciting, fun, and fulfilling. I'll share what I know with you so you can create a thriving, sustainable organization. We'll look at all kinds of aspects of nonprofit management, including the most common pitfalls to avoid, as well as the best-kept secret about how to run a smart and compassionate nonprofit, and that's to run it like a for-profit business. Many people hear the word "nonprofit" and immediately assume that because it's not making a profit, it's not a real business. This couldn't be further from the truth. Nonprofits need to bring in revenue just like for-profit businesses do, in order to pay their expenses. Expenses for nonprofits include all of the expenses for-profits have, but instead of making a product or providing a service people pay for, nonprofits often provide services for small or no fees. Therefore, they need to be smart about finding revenue, finding the right people, saving on expenses, and utilizing partners, all of which for-profit businesses do well. In the following pages, we'll look at those successes to find the best ways of managing your organization like a business and setting it up for success. So let's go on this adventure together. Let's take the passion in your heart and the smarts in your head to turn what you've only dreamed of into reality.

CHAPTER 2

More Alike than Different

"I can do things you cannot.
You can do things I cannot.
Together we can do great things."

—MOTHER THERESA

I was supposed to be the Chief Executive Officer of The Hershey Company. At least, I'm pretty sure that's what my grandfather had in mind when I started getting straight As early on, took leadership positions in high school, and declared management as my college major. My grandfather, Richard A. Zimmerman, was a successful businessman who had climbed the corporate ladder and made his way to President and Chief Executive Officer of what was, at the time, Hershey Foods Corporation (now known as The Hershey Company). Grandpa was my intellectual and moral hero. He was a brilliant man who had worked hard and steadily to get where he was. He was always humble, never touting his own achievements, and always impressing upon the family that no person is better than another. He made a point to make sure every one of the company's employees, from the factory line workers to the vice presidents, knew their job mattered.

I wanted to be just like him.

As the first-born grandchild, I was the first one to finish college and the only one interested in business. If I'd followed in his footsteps, I know that Grandpa would have been my greatest champion, best source of advice, and dedicated mentor. And maybe things would have played out the way he had hoped if I hadn't been such a bleeding heart—or perhaps if I were slightly less bull-headed. But there was this other thing gnawing at me that kept me from embracing the corporate scene: I had a heart for service, and I had fallen in love with the world of nonprofits.

It turns out that I am very much like my grandfather. I have his ability to nap anytime, anywhere, and the sarcasm he was known for. I also got his penchant for being organized, his attention to detail, and his work ethic—work always done before play. I like to think I got his honesty and integrity (I am a horrible liar), his ability to recognize the good in everyone, and his genuine and generous spirit. I also got my brains from him, although his mind for finance was sharper than mine will ever be.

Most of all, I hope I got his kindness. It's been five years since he passed, and I still hear stories of his acts of kindness, most of which I never even knew about. I know for sure that I got his desire to help others. But that's also where we differed. As a young college student, I was sure the only path to helping others was through grassroots work in the nonprofit industry. My grandfather asked me repeatedly why I wanted to go into the world of nonprofits. He believed whole-heartedly in my ability to do anything I put my mind to, but he often tried to change my mind by reminding me that "corporations do a lot of good work too." I heard him, but I didn't want to be stuck behind a desk writing checks as my only means to help people. I wanted to be on the ground, hands-on. I wanted to get into the trenches with those in need.

Helping people has been a part of my life as long as I can remember. I grew up watching my grandparents and parents consistently show benevolence to others, whether it was cooking for someone recovering from a health crisis or giving another kid a ride to soccer or band practice. My grandparents were able to give generously to many causes locally, nationally, and even internationally. I was raised going to church each Sunday, watching my offering go into the plate. Seventh grade brought confirmation at church and a host of service projects that led me to continue volunteering through high school, usually as an aide or helper at the elementary school. I even spent a summer volunteering at the local hospital, though I never did learn my way around that humongous jungle.

It helped that I found like-minded friends. One friend, in particular, was a loyal volunteer to an elementary school teacher as well as to the local library. (As giving as I'd like to say I was, I often found it disappointing as a kid when she couldn't play because it was library day!)

All of this was very relevant and pertinent to my path of service, but my most defining moments came on those two service trips to Nicaragua through Bucknell University my junior and senior years. It was a shock to me that I even volunteered for that first trip, since I was very much a homebody and attended a college only 90 minutes from home.

11

I remember the moment I realized I was considering going to Nicaragua, a third world country with plenty of weird stuff to scare me away. I was sitting in chapel service on a fall Sunday morning in 1999, listening to guest speakers from an organization in Nicaragua explain how they were helping the local people recover from Hurricane Mitch in 1998. Whether you're religious or spiritual, or perhaps neither, I can only explain that moment as one in which a voice (presumably God) spoke to me and said, "You're going to Nicaragua."

Me? What? I physically whipped my head around, wondering where in the world that came from. Hershey, Pennsylvania, was and is a small town. Though famous for our chocolate, we were still quite quaint and insulated from most of the troubles of the world. I was not a fan of leaving home, camping, or roughing it in any way, and I had certainly never considered going to a third world country. Yet the voice persisted, and I listened.

I spent the rest of that semester and the first half of the next getting ready for my trip. That required extra immunizations, anti-malarial medication, and lots of learning about what we were going to be seeing there. I often found myself thinking, "What am I doing? I still have time to back out." But the day of departure came, and by nightfall I was in Nicaragua being briefed on scorpions, dengue fever, and the unreliable electricity and water we would be experiencing throughout the week. Oh, and don't forget the killer bees. But don't worry—if they swarm, just run to the shade because they go toward the light (don't quote me on this—it could be the opposite, the specifics are a bit fuzzy). Um, what? All I kept thinking was, "How can I get back to the airport as soon as possible? I'm so out of here."

12

That night, I showered with a large spider, of whom I was not a fan. At first, it was hard to remember the rule that toilet paper could not go into the toilet but had to be in a trash can next to the toilet because the septic tank could not take toilet paper. I quickly remembered once I had to reach into the toilet and retrieve it.

The next morning, I covered myself in bug spray, since I was deathly afraid of mosquito bites. We were all taking anti-malarial medication in case we got bitten by a mosquito carrying malaria, but there were no medications or vaccines for dengue fever, which I had read about in a John Grisham book. It was a lot to take in, but as beans and rice became common breakfast items and fried plantains showed up regularly at lunch, I became amazed by how quickly we as humans physically and emotionally adapt to situations.

Spoiler alert: despite the challenges and icky stuff, I survived the trip and went a second time the following year. In addition to the reality of no soccer balls, I had several other life-changing moments that led me down the path to nonprofits. For example, we worked in what had been a barren field but had become temporary (and eventually permanent) housing to the residents from the neighborhoods that had surrounded Lake Managua in the wake of Hurricane Mitch. The government had moved the residents and given them black tarps for shelter. Black tarps. I say that again because Nicaragua is in Central America, like, near the equator. Black tarps. Some lucky ones had one-room cinder block homes. There was no electricity and no running water. We assisted in the free medical clinic and helped start the process of building a new clinic—mixing cement by hand was no small feat, but those Nicaraguan women rocked every batch. I came home with a new appreciation for cement trucks, and to this day, when I pass one on the street, I give a little nod. I will never take things like that for granted.

One day we had the opportunity to tour another city, where we ate as a group in a cafe right off the sidewalk. As I was finishing my meal, a little boy came into the restaurant and stood next to me. He was wearing what appeared to be a hand-me-down brown uniform. I hadn't noticed that I'd left some chicken on my drumstick, and he asked me if he could have it. I was so taken aback that I gave it to him, no questions asked. I couldn't believe a child off the street was asking for my leftovers. Moments later, I was scolded because what I thought was a moment of charity could have put our entire group in danger. If there were other kids hanging around who found out I'd given one of them food, they could have mobbed us and potentially hurt us or others. I had never, ever considered that fact. I was completely naive to this type of hunger, this type of life.

That moment has never left my soul.

As a junior at Bucknell, I had declared myself a management and Spanish double major. Upon my return from that first trip to Nicaragua, I maintained my majors but committed myself to looking for jobs in the nonprofit sector rather than the corporate firms so many of my classmates were clamoring for.

So while my classmates were going on interviews and internships and being courted with fancy dinners, I searched high and low for a way to help. I landed on AmeriCorps, so often described as the domestic version of the Peace Corps, and spent a year living in Northern Virginia teaching English as a Second Language (ESL) to adults. It was perfect. I'd always had a desire to teach, but knew I wasn't cut out to be an elementary school teacher.

Teaching English as a Second Language to adults was one of the most rewarding times of my life. I loved watching the metaphorical lightbulbs come on as students finally understood a new phrase or used a new word for the first time. And speaking of grassroots, we were. We were housed in an old, all-purpose room of a dilapidated school where only one computer had internet access. If you needed to use the microwave, you had to yell, "Microwave!" first to let everyone know to save their work in case there was a power surge. It wasn't glamorous, but I was in love.

I stayed on for two more years. I still taught in the classroom, but I also got to oversee day-to-day program management. I became involved in fundraising, training and managing volunteers, and extra duties, of which there are always a plethora in nonprofits (think of moving tons of books and helping to run the annual book sale, cleaning the office microwave and fridge, and packing and unpacking for an office move ourselves). As first gigs out of college go, mine was exactly what I wanted.

Upon marrying and relocating, I found another mission-based organization I loved. A nonprofit, yes, but a coalition supported by the local medical school and multiple project grants. I served as the Assistant Director for the Consortium for Infant and Child Health at Eastern Virginia Medical School in Norfolk, Virginia. We focused on bringing together groups of stakeholders (those with an interest in a project or

15

subject) in different areas of children's health. It was grass-roots organizing at its best, and it was invigorating work that showed me the power of working together and getting everyone's buy-in to turn ideas into successful initiatives.

Following that and a move back north to be closer to family, I worked briefly in public health at our local children's hospital and then subsequently went back to teaching English as a Second Language to adults, including training teachers who did so.

And then it happened: motherhood.

Motherhood has, hands-down, been the best, worst, hardest, most rewarding job I've ever had. Some might say it's the ultimate nonprofit job. Raising small humans to be good people is, after all, a clear way to make a strong difference in our society. Motherhood, however, also has a distinct way of blurring the lines between who we are, what we were before children, and what we will be again.

As a way to maintain a small hand in the nonprofit world, I worked very part-time for several organizations writing grants over the course of the next eight years or so. Grant writing in itself is a necessary nonprofit skill set that we'll explore in an upcoming chapter. For me, it was simply a vehicle to continue to help others while I was raising children. It wasn't where my heart was. My heart still belonged to direct service, grassroots work.

As my young children became school-aged children, I found myself with slightly more time. I have since worked with two small, startup nonprofits, both under 10 years old and focused in one way or another on mental health. I even shared my story publicly of living a successful life with mental health challenges, namely anxiety and depression. I managed programs, volunteers, and theater shows. I wrote more grants, met with stakeholders, and successfully obtained funding. These particular career moves were very rewarding, heart-warming, feel-good opportunities. They also allowed me to watch people in the processes of starting nonprofit organizations, revealing to me the ways that the process could be made easier, that errors could be avoided, and that there were many times when following a model makes more sense than reinventing the wheel. Learning this allowed me to realize that education is a true passion of mine, and educating others on how to start a nonprofit could allow me to make my bigger impact.

This is what brings me to you. This book is my chance to share the knowledge and wisdom my experiences afforded me, so that you and your nonprofit can reach further into the world and so that you can be successful by using both your head and your heart. I want to empower you, and other difference makers like you, to reach your highest potential. I want to guide you through a process that will enable you to start, manage, and grow a healthy, successful nonprofit, one built on a solid foundation of business principles and compassion that will expand your difference-making impact beyond your imagination. Ready? Let's get started.

CHAPTER 3

Let's Get Started

"Doing good not only feels good,
it leads to more good."

—KAREN SALMANSOHN

Most of us come to nonprofit service with stars in our eyes and a dream in our hearts. Dreams can be powerful fuel for action—but without common-sense business practices to accompany them, they make for a less-than-stable foundation for your nonprofit venture. I once worked for an early childhood education nonprofit that had an admirable mission, but hit upon hard times because it was run by impulse and heart alone, rather than sound business principles. The director announced that all of us three employees were going to have to be furloughed (go without a salary) until we found additional funding. Though I was working in the nonprofit sector, that was still my job, and I still needed income.

Too often, nonprofits don't see the importance of bringing in enough revenue to cover their expenses and fulfill their missions. Nonprofits cannot fulfill their missions without covering all of their expenses, including salaries and then some. Another nonprofit I came to know couldn't finish paying an employee the rest of her last paycheck after she resigned until some grant money came through, grant money that was not meant for salaries. Therefore, once that money was used to complete payroll, the organization was going to be in debt because that money was required to be spent on programs, not salaries. This is irresponsible, and it's also unethical. Neither of these scenarios would fly in the for-profit business world.

No matter what kind of nonprofit you're planning to launch, you will encounter challenges and obstacles—or F*&king Opportunities for Growth (FOGS) as Lisa Wade, author of *Real. Big. Love.: A Difference Maker's Guide to Gain Greater Clarity, Energy, and Impact for Your Cause and Life,* so lovingly calls them. The nonprofit industry isn't as cutthroat as one might call the finance or technology industry, but it is competitive and complex, particularly when it comes to funding. There are so many necessary and worthy causes in our world.

That said, how do you convince people to support your organization? What may be of utmost importance and interest to one person—to you—may be of no relevance to another. Hunger? Homelessness? Clean water? You'll need to learn to tell a compelling story. As nonprofit owners, it's incumbent upon us to convince others to believe in and contribute to our particular cause.

Something I've learned and seen time and again is that, although money might seem difficult to come by, the funding is there, and plentifully so, if you look in the right places and speak to the right people. The importance of networking cannot be understated. Building relationships with other people and organizations, which I'll teach you how to do, are invaluable ways to locate the resources you need, as are creativity and willingness to try new things.

Nonprofits commonly have difficulty managing another, and arguably most important, resource: their people. When running a nonprofit, it's hard to make decisions about when to bring people on, how to compensate them, and how to manage not only employees but also volunteers. Volunteers are the backbone of the nonprofit industry, serving in roles from office assistant to program director to, in some cases, executive director. Some nonprofits rely solely on the work of volunteers, whereas others use volunteers sparingly. Some organizations use volunteers where, as they say, the rubber meets the road, or to provide the actual service being offered in areas such as tutoring, teaching, or delivering meals. Volunteers are a tremendous asset and also a liability. Managing them requires special forethought and diligence.

In this book, we'll be looking at how to manage volunteers versus employees. Those on the payroll must also be compensated properly (as evidenced in the above example), which is often difficult on shoestring budgets. Creativity, flexibility, and knowing how to leverage assets are all key. Documented policies and procedures are also extremely important in dealing with people, paid or not.

Burnout is another very real potential pitfall for most nonprofits. Nonprofit work is rewarding for sure, but it is also often very hard either physically or mentally and very time-consuming. Progress can be slow. It's an arena in which it's easy to take three steps forward and two steps back. It's not for the faint of heart, and persistence is paramount. Nonprofit employees also often fill multiple roles or wear multiple hats within the organization, and that can lead to weariness in maintaining enthusiasm for the cause. While it's true that we can find fulfillment in serving others, it is also true that we cannot take care of others if we don't take care of ourselves first.

Remember that safety speech you hear every time you board an airplane? They remind us to put on our own oxygen masks before helping others. To some people, including parents and caregivers, this sounds counterintuitive. Our instinct is to take care of others first. But if we pass out from oxygen deprivation, we are of no help to anyone, including our children.

The same holds true for service professions, including nonprofits. We cannot serve others if we are coming from a place of need ourselves. We cannot sacrifice ourselves to save others or we will be of no help to anyone. The good news is the issue of burnout can be greatly remedied with some thoughtful strategies surrounding proper staffing, role selecting, and flexibility, all of which are essential in building a solid foundation for a nonprofit.

Another important challenge for nonprofits is what I like to call the "We're just a nonprofit" mentality. So often, nonprofits are caught in the cycle of trying to share their stories with others to garner support for their cause while simultaneously projecting an air of ignorance. All too many nonprofit managers and directors make the mistake of not approaching their organizations as proper businesses, so to speak, either because they feel they aren't there yet or because they don't want to be associated with the perceived greedy or money-hungry attributes of the for-profit agenda.

Don't fall for this. We've been led to believe, throughout the past several decades, that corporate America's for-profit businesses equal greedy, ruthless, and bad, whereas non-profit businesses equal heart-warming, awe-inspiring, and good. The problem here is, carried forward, that belief means heart-warming and good cannot, by definition, mean making money, operating like a business, or utilizing the same resources a for-profit would.

Believe it or not, this is a myth, albeit an understandable one. It is often easier, administratively-speaking, to get on the ground and help others directly without the red tape of large businesses and the concern with bottom-line profits. Putting ideas into action is often less complicated (barring the factor of necessary resources) for nonprofits because there are fewer departments and people to pass things through. But that doesn't mean that nonprofits cannot and should not take pages from the playbooks of big business.

There is a way to marry the thought processes from the two that can be mutually beneficial to both, which is a nod to the title of this book. Nonprofits must make money (using your head) to serve others (with your heart). Gregory Demetriou, CEO of Lorraine Gregory Communications, said in his article Why New Nonprofits Fail, "Every time someone decides they should address a cause, a disease, or a community injustice, they become focused on having an impact. That is wonderful on its own, but that zeal needs to be supported in a meaningful way by human physical work and by money. One without the other just will not work. New nonprofits must act like a corporate startup."[1]

In other words, in order to make money, nonprofits must

run themselves like the businesses they are. They must have a proper foundation, consistent procedures and protocols, and proper personnel management. I've witnessed what may appear to be insignificant mistakes, such as less than professional etiquette, sloppy communication, or even lax dress codes, but are actually serious gaffes because they don't project a professional business mindset. Missteps like these can cause others to question an organization's mission, dedication, or legitimacy, and those misunderstandings are much more difficult to remedy than simply putting your best foot forward in the first place. After all, if you don't put any effort into your appearance or your grammar, how much attention do you pay to your accounting or your expenses? The leap is not a big one.

So yes, there are challenges in running any nonprofit, and each organization faces unique obstacles. Some of them are easily remedied. Many can even be avoided altogether if the organization is built on a solid foundation. Starting and running a nonprofit won't always be rainbows and unicorns, but there are also substantial rewards, not the least of which is the sense of personal fulfillment.

Giving to others has the unique ability to fill each of us even as we fill each other up. Helping one another is one of life's greatest gifts, and it is in the giving that we ourselves receive. We feel accomplished, warm, and have a sense of purpose. Knowing we may have made life just slightly easier for another provides hope and peace. As great teacher Ram Dass has said, "We are all just walking each other home." What a beautiful analogy for the journey we are all on together. And what a magical way to live a life—by making each other's path easier.

It's an incredible journey you've decided to undertake, and I would love to accompany you in making your dream a reality. During this journey, we are going to go methodically through the most important and relevant nonprofit topics and the best ways for you to handle them. Where needed, I will provide specific steps for you to follow, actions to take, and resources to help along the way. At the end of each chapter, I'll provide you with the most salient points and ways to implement each of them. We'll talk about the pitfalls to avoid, ways to make things easier, and mistakes that have already been made so that you don't have to make them. You will not walk away feeling like you have to reinvent the wheel or take a shot in the dark to get started. Topics we will cover include:

- Defining your success based on the successful creation of your mission
- How to begin fundraising and get off the ground
- The legalities of creating an organization, including necessary business practices
- Creating and working with a Board of Directors
- Setting goals and strategic planning for the future as well as growth and succession
- Staffing, both paid and unpaid
- Communication inside and outside the organization
- Efficiency and effectiveness
- Burnout
- Pitfalls and troubleshooting

Each chapter contains examples, stories, and input from successful founders, directors, and executives in the field. We'll take it step-by-step, together, to determine how you can expand your impact, help more people, and fulfill your mission. I'll have your back as you digest all of the information to see how it can help the unique organization that you are ready to build and grow. I'll break things down, point you in the right direction, and help you become successful at beginning and running your own nonprofit. You've got this!

CHAPTER 4

Where Do I Start?:

Getting Legal, Defining Success, and Finding Funding

Start by doing what's necessary;
then do what's possible;
and suddenly you are doing the impossible.

—ST. FRANCIS OF ASSISI

You've got your idea, your enthusiasm, and passion to move forward. You're ready to move forward, but how? Of course, there are a lot of things to think about, including legalities, forms, and even big, scary business words. There's funding and mission and employees and...

Before you begin to worry though, let's start with something very basic. One of the first things you need to think about and act on is finding out whether someone else is already doing the thing that you want to do.

The nonprofit sector (also sometimes referred to as the voluntary sector or charitable sector, among other names) is a very full and busy part of the worldwide economy. It might surprise you—it surprised me!—to find out that there are over 1.5 million nonprofit organizations registered in the US alone (grantspace.org/resources/knowledge-base/number-of-nonprofits-in-the-u-s/accessed 5/15/19). These organizations have come into existence to fill gaps in services that exist between what our private businesses and our government provide.

Chances are, you're impacted by at least one of these organizations every day. Do you listen to NPR on your drive to work? Do your children go to a charter school? Do you have a pet from the Humane Society? Perhaps you scour thrift shops for good deals, or frequent the library, or attend a place of worship. These are all examples of different types of nonprofits. Our government categorizes nonprofits depending on their missions, and those categories determine many financial and organizational rules for each nonprofit. For the purposes of this book, we're focusing on the most common category of nonprofits, the one you're considering starting. That is the 501(c)(3) classification, otherwise known as a charitable organization.

When we think of charitable organizations, some of the most common things that usually come to mind are food banks, homeless shelters, and larger organizations like the American Red Cross or the United Way. All of these are 501(c)(3) organizations, which the Internal Revenue Service (IRS) defines as organizations that benefit the public, a specific group of people, or the members of the nonprofit themselves. "Charitable organizations" also include things like arts and culture organizations, schools, some hospitals, and private foundations. Although we will touch on some of these organizations and you may see examples from them used in this book, we will not specifically cover the financial and organizational details of groups like these because we want to focus on the organization you want to start.

Is My Organization Needed?

This is one of the most important points of this chapter. Before you begin the process of forming your nonprofit, you must find out if such an organization already exists. As I mentioned, the nonprofit sector is very full, and people have come up with varied and unique solutions to solve societal problems. There are several factors to consider, including competition, the economy, and the needs of your community.

First of all, does any other organization exist in your geographical area that does what you'd like to do? Do they do it exactly the way you'd like to? Do you have a specific spin on an existing concept that would differentiate you enough from other similar organizations so you wouldn't be competing against one another?

In the for-profit world, you wouldn't set up a business that has lots of competition in its immediate area or marketplace. Nonprofits must do the same. Most times, you will not want to duplicate something that already exists. Even so, there are times in which more space exists in the market you're aiming for, in which case you might be able to add your organization to the community or explore the possibility of a partnership with another organization. For example, many communities have homeless shelters, and many communities have more than one. But if there are more than one, they are often differentiated by things like gender or operating hours. If you live in a community that has a shelter that serves men, perhaps you need one that serves women. Perhaps you have one that is open overnight but not during the day. That is a gap you could fill. You simply do not want to do be in direct competition with something that already exists. That won't benefit you or the clients you want to serve.

So how do you do that? One of the easiest ways is to start with a Google (or your own favorite web browser) search. Start by searching key words about your idea in your area. For example, if you want to feed children who are hungry, begin by searching for hunger statistics in your area. Follow that with a search for local programs that provide food. Visit websites of local churches or schools to see if they already have feeding programs. You may even want to contact school district personnel like counselors, nurses, and teachers to see if they know of local programs. Some other good resources when looking for organizations that do particular kinds of charitable work include CharityNavigator.org, guidestar.org, and VolunteerMatch.org. These websites allow nonprofits to register themselves so they are searchable by what they do, where they are located, and whether they are looking for volunteers. And it's always a good idea to talk to those around you, in your community, and in the subject area in which you're interested.

Secondly, an important factor to consider is your local economy. Will you be offering a service for free or charging potential clients? Are those potential clients in your area able to pay for your services? Is your local area already saturated with other nonprofits frequently asking your community members for donations? If so, it might be difficult for you to appeal to those people to support your cause financially. Perhaps your community is going through a difficult economic time and may not be able to help support you at all. These are things to consider.

For the past several years, my daughter, E., has run her own lemonade stand. It's kind of a rite of passage for many children, but in this case, my daughter's big heart led her to introduce a twist. Since age six, she has given her lemonade stand proceeds to different causes, one of which was sick children at our local children's hospital. Let's take her lemonade stand as a small example of a starting nonprofit. Let's call it Lemon Aid for Little Ones (LALO).

The first time my daughter wanted to have a stand, she wanted to give the profits partially to our local children's hospital which is part of the larger Children's Miracle Network, and partially to our local library. Though a very simple business model for a nonprofit, I still had to think about the things mentioned above: Was there a need in the community? Was there space in our local economy? Would we be competing with anyone else? Of course this was a quick assessment—there's almost always room for a kid's lemonade stand in small neighborhoods across the country, and there is usually little competition. After all, people tend to be generous when they see children trying to sell lemonade on the street—the cuteness factor is big!

Since there are lots of groups in our area who fundraise for our children's hospital, we decided together that her proceeds would go directly to the hospital's Child Life program, which provides a playroom, toys, and activities to engage children over a long hospital stay. That differentiated us slightly from the larger fundraisers that raise money for the broader Children's Miracle Network at Penn State Hershey Children's Hospital.

The next question was whether or not there would be interest in our lemonade stand, since so many groups fund-raise in our area. Since my daughter was only six years old and we live on a cul- de-sac in a neighborhood that doesn't get any foot traffic, it was clear we wouldn't get customers without my engaging friends and family. But I also knew that those friends and family would be likely to fork over $.50 for a cup of lemonade, so she would have customers for her stand and would, at the very least, make a few dollars. I also agreed to provide her starting capital (cups, lemonade, change) without repayment; therefore, she didn't have to ask others for dona-tions to get started.

With LALO, it was easy to decide we could make a lem-onade stand go because even if there were other lemonade stands in our area, the market was not saturated with them. Plus, people like to buy and drink lemonade, and buying one cup of lemonade does not prohibit them from buying another from another stand, unlike, say, enrolling in an English as a Second Language class from one program, which might pre-clude you from enrolling in other due to time constraints, cost, or the rules of the first program. Therefore, a compli-cated needs assessment of whether our area needed a lemon-ade stand was not necessary. It's important to note, though, that even if you find that no other organization in your area serves the need you have in mind, you must take at least some time to assess the immediate needs of your community.

It's possible that no organization like yours exists simply

because there's no market for it. For example, if you want to start a nonprofit that focuses on literacy and teaching people to read, what's the average educational level in your area? If the majority of people are high school or college graduates, there might not be a true need for a such a service. However, if you live in an economically depressed area in which people quit school to work prior to graduation, you might have a niche to fulfill that would elevate both the educational level and perhaps the economy of the area. On the other hand, if you are in an economically disadvantaged area and are interested in starting a nonprofit theater or dance company, that may not meet the needs of the community. The community may be in greater need of housing, hunger relief, or after-school resources.

The easiest way to assess the needs of your community is to talk to people. Ask around at the local spots, coffee shops, grocery stores, libraries, and PTO meetings, just to name a few. Find out what others see as the needs of your area. You can even create short questionnaires to get others' input. You can interview community members and leaders, and even people who run businesses (both for-profit and non) in your area by asking them questions like:

- What do you see as the biggest need in our community?
- What types of goods/services have you heard community members request?
- If you had a magic wand for our community, what is the biggest problem you would fix?

You can find additional resources on Needs Assessments in the Resources page of this book. Gather as much information as you can before determining whether your idea is indeed necessary in your area. And never discount the idea of partnering with another organization, for- profit or nonprofit. Partnering with another organization does not mean your idea was not good enough or new enough. It simply means you're going to work together to serve your potential clients in the most efficient and effective way possible (more on that later!).

One example of a great partnership is the Family Literacy Program at the Literacy Council of Northern Virginia (lcnv. org). The Literacy Council partners with local elementary schools to provide Family Literacy Classes. While teachers from the Literacy Council teach parents English, childcare workers, provided by the school, work with the children on the same content, including topics like community and health. The elementary schools are responsible for providing proper classrooms, childcare providers, and snacks for the children. The Literacy Council is responsible for providing English teachers with content for the parents and children, and pre- and post-testing of the adult students.

This partnership uses the best assets of both organizations to bring together a program that benefits the entire community. The school already has a place to hold classes and access to adults who have been cleared by security as well as the families to populate the program, and the Literacy Council has teachers trained in adult education who can provide proper materials at the appropriate level for the students. All parties work together to bring the adults and children together for activities throughout the semesters. By educating these families, the community gains better educated adults who can attain better jobs which leads to families being able to sustain themselves more effectively and take advantage of the other services offered in the community. Children are enriched with friendships and trusted adults as well as introduction to the school system before they reach school-age. The partnership is a win-win for everyone, which is something to keep in mind for your organization.

What Is Success?

Now that you've determined that your idea is a great one that is going to fill an important hole in your community, you need to think about what success is going to look like for you. Success is not an all-or-nothing proposition, and it's defined differently for different people and organizations. When E. first started her lemonade stand, my goal of success for her was just to make a nominal amount of money and learn about what it's like to put some work into something and donate the proceeds to others. But if we were turning LALO into an actual nonprofit, a measure of success could be a monetary goal for donation that grows each year.

In your case, one measure of success could be simply that you make enough revenue to continue providing the service you want to provide. After all, non-profit work is hard and often tedious, and your biggest aim may be to simply continue what you're doing, continue to serve. Winston Churchill said, "Success is not final; failure isn't fatal: It is the courage to continue that counts." Continuing despite failures and challenges is a tremendous measure of success, and a fabulous goal!

Another way to measure your success might be through

the number of people you serve or the number of ways your organization serves. Perhaps your goal is to grow each year to provide slightly more services for slightly more people or provide new and different services. LALO could expand to operate more than once a year or in multiple locations. It could begin to offer more than just lemonade and try to create other sources of revenue.

You might also define your success by how quickly you can work yourself out of a job. After all, if you are aiming to fill a void and you do that well enough, there may come a time when your organization is no longer needed. Instead of seeing that as the end of something you set out to do, it could be seen as the accomplishment of your goal or even a springboard for a new service or mission. With respect to new things, perhaps your definition of success will be dependent upon how well you adapt and how flexible your organization is in fulfilling your community's differing needs. It's unlikely that the Child Life program at our children's hospital would grow to not need any additional funding in the future, but it is possible that LALO could adjust its mission to fund two areas such as Child Life and research or Child Life and the Ronald McDonald House, which provides housing for families who have children staying in the hospital.

One organization that has done a tremendous job of adapting its definition of success and meeting the community's changing needs is the Consortium for Infant and Child Health (CINCH) in Norfolk, VA (cinchcoalition. org). CINCH is unique in that it is a consortium of different stakeholders housed as part of the Eastern Virginia Medical School. It does the majority of its project work through grant funding and forms working groups of community stakeholders to determine the best ways to complete projects. That allows the group to continuously assess the community's needs and adjust its programs accordingly.

Back in 2007, CINCH was focused on several key areas, including asthma, obesity, health disparities, immunizations, and enrolling children in Virginia's free child health insurance program. As the enrollment rate in the health insurance program climbed, the program met its goals, and state funding and the working group's focus changed. One program, which was at first tightly focused on asthma education and management, now encompasses broader respiratory health efforts such as non-smoking initiatives, clean air, and most recently, anti-vaping campaigns and strategies. It's a great example of a nonprofit adapting to fulfill the changing needs of its community.

CINCH is one of the most effective and efficient nonprofits of which I've been honored to be a part. The most important thing to learn from CINCH is that success can be constantly redefined depending on the needs of your community. It's up to you to decide how you will define success for your organization, and to look for how that definition can evolve over time. For now, know that how you define success will be an integral part of how you determine your organization's mission, which we'll cover in the next chapter.

Speaking of the next chapter, we're not quite there yet, dear reader, so if you need a breath or a stretch, please take one. We'll tackle a lot of information in this book that may seem daunting at times, but it will indeed be relevant to you if you can hang in there!

Where Is the Money Coming From?

One fundamental piece of getting a nonprofit off the ground is funding. How much funding will you need? Where will it come from? How will you sustain it? Does your initial funding money need to be paid back to someone?

These are all intimidating questions, but there are plenty of manageable solutions. In an ideal world, you would have a nice little (or big) pot of money you've been saving for your cause over the course of several years. But that's in an ideal world where you had mapped out your entire life's plan, knowing that you were going to start a nonprofit someday. Unlikely, right? For most people, yes, totally. Which begs the question, what are the other options?

The reality is that even if you start small, perhaps in your own home without an office space and it's only you and perhaps a few volunteers, you will still incur costs, so you have to be smart. Simple things like letterhead, printing, postage, equipment, and even mileage reimbursement for travel will be required. You will also incur fees for filing applications with your state and the IRS. The best way to begin thinking about how much you'll need is to estimate a startup budget.

I know the word budget is scary, but we'll take it step by step. Your startup budget should include everything you need to start your organization, from equipment (perhaps a computer, phone, printer) to supplies (paper, business cards, ink), and filing fees. You'll want to include insurance, rental space (if needed), startup materials you will need to actually provide your services (do you need books to teach, storage or containers in which to organize, an initial supply of food or donation supplies?) and lots of other things that will inevitably come up as you go (for this reason, always estimate on the high side—it's always better to overestimate and save money than find yourself in need of emergency funds).

Your startup budget will be different than the general operating budget you will create each year. You could include the first several months of operations to get your organization off the ground, but you don't want to combine an annual budget with this startup budget. It will be important to differentiate between the two so that you understand what your initial costs will be versus what your continuous operating costs will be.

In the case of both budgets as well as special budgets for programs, it is vitally important to be aware of what things cost. This seems like an obvious point to make, but inevitably, things end up costing us more than we anticipate, and that goes for all types of businesses in all types of industries. Therefore, it's necessary to research multiple outlets for prices of supplies. Just as you would search for the best prices for things you buy at home, you will want to do the same for your organization. Even if you don't choose the cheapest items available (which is not always a good idea anyway, depending on quality), it's crucial to know in what range you should be estimating your costs. Always estimate higher rather than lower.

One of the reasons it's important to separate a startup budget is that unless you have a magic pile of money saved for your new adventure, you're going to have to find someone or something to help you with funding. Those investors are going to want to know how much you need and where it will be going in as much detail as possible. You're going to have to be ready to make a passionate, solid case that your new nonprofit is going to provide a valuable service to your community with this money. You will have to not only show your compassion but also your well- thought-out business plans. This "pitch" to potential donors or investors needs to demonstrate that this idea is necessary, worthwhile, and will ultimately be successful.

Once you feel you have a solid budget and can speak intelligently and convincingly about your idea, you need to think about who might be willing to listen to your pitch and potentially help. A good pitch should include several elements we'll cover later, including your mission and vision, your goals, your strategies for reaching them, and the resources you currently have available to you. This is one of many important times you're going to need to sell your organization, so to speak, to convince others that it's worth funding. So your pitch needs to be passionate, with real human interest, as well as professional in both content and presentation. Think for-profit business! This is not a time to be casual, informal, or even dressed down. This is the time to make your best impression. You will then want to make sure to follow up with any potential investors—we'll talk about that when we cover communication.

There are two options for finding financial help. You can seek out investors who are willing to provide you with funds and then get paid back when your organization becomes successful, or you can find people willing to donate without needing or wanting to recuperate their costs. In layman's terms, donations come with no strings attached—they are given to your cause without expectation of repayment, and usually those donations are tax deductions for the donor. For example, I supplied the startup capital for my daughter's first lemonade stand. If LALO is going to be a nonprofit, I might be willing to do that again, or I might want her to find someone else, such as an investor, willing to help. Investors may be willing to provide you more funding initially, but will most likely work out a plan with you for them to get repaid their initial funds plus interest.

The decision between the two may come down to what's available to you in your community. The decision could also be determined by your own moral compass. If you feel confident about accepting donations, knowing that your organization may not become successful, donations may be the way to go. Still, if you feel ultimately responsible for the money others put into your cause and its success, you may be more comfortable making a commitment to pay someone back. If this is the case, remember that if your organization isn't successful, you will still owe that money.

One important thing to note is that there are procedures to follow in filing your nonprofit status with the IRS and your state. There may be times where you are in financial limbo and trying to obtain startup funding while awaiting these determinations. During this time, as long as your exemption status is pending (you've started the process and applied and are awaiting response), you may collect donations from individuals. Those donations will then be deductible for the donor when your tax-exempt status is approved. But if the exemption is denied and you have already received contributions, those won't be deductible to the donor, and you may be responsible for income tax on that money.

One area of funding that I did not mention is grant

funding. While this can be an important and helpful source of income, foundations and corporations will rarely provide startup grants to an organization not yet recognized by the IRS as tax-exempt. Therefore, if you can find ways to fund, in the very least, your filing status on your own, you could avoid unnecessary stress and potential legal complications. Once your status is approved, your options for funding will open up to include potential startup grants.

One final alternative to obtaining startup funding would also allow you to avoid being in the actual business of running a nonprofit financially. Finding a fiscal sponsor for your idea would mean that the project you're dreaming of would become a sponsored program of another already established nonprofit. This harkens back to the idea of partnership in that this fiscal sponsor organization would be responsible for the bureaucratic and legal matters you might not want to focus on day after day. You would be responsible for your program's budget and activities, but your filing status would fall underneath the fiscal sponsor, and you would not have to pursue the entire startup process. There are advantages to this arrangement, particularly if you're just starting out and want to gauge whether your idea is plausible or you want to test a smaller version of it. Fiscal sponsors provide an established organizational structure, bookkeeping, human resources, and other types of expertise. Making an arrangement like this can provide you the time and space to experiment with your idea and determine whether you want to move forward to create your own 501(c)(3) identity.

There are cautions to be taken as well. The mission of the organization serving as your fiscal sponsor should be aligned with your mission. For example, if you're aiming to provide food for children at an after-school program, you wouldn't want to approach a museum or theater as a fiscal sponsor. You will need approval from the Board of Directors of the fiscal sponsor organization, and you will need to sign a contract with the organization detailing both parties' responsibilities.

There will most likely be a fee you will have to pay to the organization for it to sponsor your project, and you will have to inform donors that in order to donate to your particular project, they must note that in the donation. It is important to be very thorough in your search for a fiscal sponsor, making sure that the two of you fit together well and all details are worked out ahead of time. A good resource for finding a fiscal sponsor is fiscalsponsordirectory.org. The National Network of Fiscal Sponsors (fiscalsponsors.org) has developed best practices for fiscal sponsorship partnerships and is also a helpful resource.

Using E.'s lemonade stand, LALO, as an example, I agreed to provide the startup funding as a donation. The startup budget was quite minimal, with costs only for supplies as I was also providing the location for the stand and overhead costs of electricity, water, etc. Cups, lemonade, or the ingredients for lemonade were the only supplies. Because E.'s lemonade stand was not becoming a nonprofit organization in itself, we did not have to file for tax-exempt statuses. We simply promised her customers that all of their money would be going directly to charity. This also meant they could not deduct the cost of any additional donations they made to our cause, but because we have very generous friends and customers, many gave extra without worrying about the tax deduction. Of course, if E. wanted to focus fully on making and selling lemonade rather than turning her idea into a full-fledged nonprofit, she could partner with another organization so that she wouldn't have to worry about filing status, determining personnel salaries, and other issues. She would want to find a partner that also had a mission to help the local children's hospital or at least a similar cause. She would not want to partner with an organization that had a completely different area of focus, such as an art museum or local PBS station.

Your Business Plan

After you've gathered all of this information and decided that you want to move forward with your organization, you will have to put together a business plan. Potential funders and stakeholders will want to see a written plan documenting what you are going to do and how you are going to do it before they will consider providing funding. This plan should be typed and printed (or sent electronically if a potential funder or stakeholder prefers) in a professional looking way with close attention to format, grammar, spelling, and typos (we'll be talking about the importance of these things in Chapter 11). Later we will also discuss strategic plans, which are very similar to business plans but not interchangeable (Chapter 10). Below are some of the items your business plan should include:

- Executive Summary
- Needs Statement (why the organization/program is needed in your community)
- Description of the program and how you will implement it

- Why your organization is best poised to implement it
- Resumes and backgrounds for people who will provide and manage the organization/services
- Three-year projections of income and expenses for the organization/program with a budget for the current year, which will most likely be your startup budget

Each of the elements of a business plan can be found in multiple resources across the internet. You will not find forms you can simply fill in to complete —you'll have to create your own document. You can search for samples of things like Executive Summaries and budget formats should you need them. An Executive Summary, for example, can be thought of as a wrap-up of what you've put in the plan, but a wrap-up that comes at the beginning. In other words, you'll want to give a brief (1–2 page) overview of what you have in your plan without going into details. You want your Executive Summary to give your potential funder, stakeholder, employee, etc., a thorough glimpse of what follows and a desire to keep reading. The other elements of your business plan should be as long as you need them to be in order to thoroughly explain your plan in as much detail as possible. You want to market and sell your organization as the best way to address this need in your community.

This was a long, in-depth chapter, my friend, but you made it. As you can see, beginning and running a nonprofit consists of many decisions your head and heart both need to weigh in on. You've got to be smart and set yourself up as if you're going to run a for-profit business, as your nonprofit will need all of the same forethought and insight. I know this all seems very overwhelming, so please know that it is completely ok to take it piece by piece until you have gotten your start. Use this list to help:

Motivations and Takeaways

- You are embarking on something awesome. Way to go, you!
- Before you go all in, make sure no one is doing what you want to do. Make sure you're bringing something unique and necessary to the table.

- Determine your definition of success while being aware that the best organizations grow and redefine success as the community's needs change.

- Create a thorough startup budget and pitch to drum up interest in your organization.

- Determine how you are going to find startup funding.

- Write a thorough and engaging business plan you can provide to potential funders, stakeholders, employees, volunteers, and board members.

- Get excited!

CHAPTER 5

The Nitty Gritty

Mission & Vision

*In the successful organization, no detail is too
small to escape close attention..*

—LOU HOLTZ

L et's take stock for a moment. You've done your research
and determined that there is a need for your nonprofit in your area. You have a plan for raising startup
funding and at least an idea of what you'll need. That's a lot
of hard work already accomplished, so give yourself a pat on
the back. Now you're ready to get into the nitty gritty. But
don't worry, it doesn't have to be tedious. You have tasks to
complete, but you can also use your creativity and your own
voice to create things the way you want them. Let's start with
the passion that brought you to this work in the first place.

Mission

Your mission statement is one the most fundamental, most used, and most effective ways of communicating what your organization does to the general public. It's the one sentence that you will refer to over and over again, not only-for explaining your organization to others but also to plan appropriately for your growth and success. For nonprofits and for-profits alike, it communicates what your organization values and tells others your long-term goals, how you're going to accomplish them, and whom you are going to affect. It will be used many times over, from your articles of incorporation and corporate documents to your marketing materials and communication tools. Simply speaking, your mission statement explains your purpose, your goals, and what you do.

Your mission will also be part of your "elevator pitch," or the 30-second explanation you would give to someone asking about your organization. It needs to be concise, precise, and easy to understand. It's common to get caught up in the idea that a mission statement should be impressive-sounding and full of big words, but that's not the case. The purpose of the mission statement is to quickly and succinctly share with others what your organization does, and sometimes why.

Every business and organization should have a mission statement—but that doesn't mean that all of them are effective, even in the for-profit world. For example, Avon (the beauty brand) once had a mission statement that began like this, "Avon's mission is focused on six core aspirations the company continually strives to achieve" and then went on for

249 additional words. Too lengthy. Avery, the company that makes widely used sticky labels, once used a mission statement that read, "To help make every brand more inspiring, and the world more intelligent." Huh? What exactly are they doing, and how are they doing it? Both companies have since changed their mission statements, but serve as good examples of what not to do when trying to write one.

Let's take a look at excerpts from three well-written and effective mission statements: one from a national nonprofit, one from a regional nonprofit, and one from a local nonprofit. See what common threads you can find among them. Can you describe what they have in common? Look particularly at their phrasing, the words they've used, and whether they are easy to understand.

1. Mission: To prevent and alleviate human suffering in the face of emergencies by mobilizing the power of volunteers and the generosity of donors.[3] (American Red Cross, redcross.org)

2. Mission: To teach adults the basic skills of reading, writing, speaking, and understanding English so they can access employment and educational opportunities and more fully and equitably participate in the community.[4] (Literacy Council of Northern Virginia, lcnv.org)

3. Mission: To provide cultural and educational opportunities to the Hershey community.[5] (The M.S. Hershey Foundation, mshersheyfoundation.org)

In the above mission statements, you can see some of the qualities I've cited. They are concise, they communicate their purposes, and they do not use flowery or complicated language. They use simple verbs to convey what each organization does and, in one case, why. As you'll notice, the mission of the American Red Cross *("To prevent and alleviate human suffering in the face of emergencies by mobilizing the power of volunteers and the generosity of donors")* also communicates how it accomplishes its goals—by mobilizing the power of volunteers and generosity of donors. That's because that phrase is integral to the purpose of the organization. In this case, the organization could not accomplish its mission without the use of volunteers and donations. Without those two things, the organization cannot translate its purpose into action. It's crucial that its mission include that qualifying phrase.

In the case of the Literacy Council of Northern Virginia *("To teach adults the basic skills of reading, writing, speaking, and understanding English so they can access employment and educational opportunities and more fully and equitably participate in the community"),* the mission explains the outcome of teaching English in terms of specific goals. Sometimes these details need to be shared in order to differentiate the organization from another in the same region that provides similar services. Or, these details need to be provided so that potential funders can immediately recognize that while the goal is certainly to educate, the purpose of educating its clients is to make them more productive members of society. This idea is greatly attractive to funders who want to see that the investment in this education is going to pay off in concrete ways. Finally, the mission statement of The M.S. Hershey Foundation *("To provide cultural and educational opportunities to the Hershey community")* is very short and precise.

It communicates the actions taken by the organization and shows that those actions cover a wide array of activities, programs, and opportunities. Someone would only need to read the mission statement to decide if that organization is of any interest not only from a potential funding/donation perspective but also as a prospective community member.

Let's create one of our own for our Lemon Aid for Little Ones (LALO). Before anything else, who do you think should be involved in creating our mission statement? The answer is those who have a stake in the development of the organization. Depending on the organization, this could include you as the founder, some board members, some potential staff members or volunteers, or some potential funders. It doesn't need to be a large number of people, but the idea is that two (or more) heads are better than one. Many times a founder of an organization has an idea of where they want to take the organization, but others can be helpful in articulating that. In the case of LALO, the logical choices would be my daughter and me, although I would most likely garner some opinions from business-minded friends, potential investors (likely family or friends), and maybe even someone from the children's hospital. It doesn't hurt to get others' input. You can always take it or leave it.

So now what do you think a good mission statement for LALO would be? We know we're going to sell lemonade (and maybe extend our offerings later on), and we know we're going to give the proceeds to Child Life at the local children's hospital. Who are we hoping to attract to our lemonade stand? What is unique about our lemonade stand as opposed to another local kid's lemonade stand? Take a minute to think about this, and we will revisit it at the end of the chapter. Remember, the point is to make the mission clear, concise, and easy to understand. When asked about the most important piece of advice she would give to someone starting a nonprofit, Tammy Hiller, professor of management in the Freeman College of Management at Bucknell University, cited clarity in mission. She advises, "Really understanding what you're trying to accomplish and articulating that well moving forward is not only key to the success of the organization but also helps to garner financial support."

Funders want to quickly and easily determine what it is you do so they can decide whether they want to become part of supporting your organization. Your mission statement is going to serve as your most frequently used and most dependable way to share what you do, keep you true to what you set out to do, and help you and others decide where you fit in the nonprofit sector.

All of this being said, is your mission statement set in stone? No! As we'll revisit again and again in this book, the most successful nonprofits are flexible and adapt to the changing needs of the communities they serve. That's why you might start out with a well-worded mission statement explaining how you're going to approach your new idea and how it will play out, and stay alert to how that might change. Many organizations create a mission statement that continues to be true for years and years. Other organizations create mission statements and never go back to reassess them. In those cases, the mission statement may or may not continue to be true, but the organization has not taken a critical look at the changing times. When you're just starting a nonprofit, you'll come up with an initial mission statement that may very well work for a few months or a few years. Yet, as time goes on, you will want to revisit your mission statement to see if it still reflects what your organization is actually doing. You may need to change a few words, or you may need to redefine your goals.

One nonprofit, Someone To Tell It To (STTIT), crafted a mission statement articulating that the organization accompanies others on a journey toward meaningful connections. That mission statement worked for about five years. Then, as time passed and the organization grew and changed, it recrafted its mission statement to read: *Someone To Tell It To cultivates meaningful relationships through compassionate listening and trains others to do the same.*[6] This more closely reflects the current activities of the organization and clearly illustrates what it sets out to do. The current mission statement is more effective in that it precisely and concisely states the organization's goal and how it plans to achieve it. The language is not flowery or complicated, it uses clear action verbs, and it mentions compassionate listening, which is a keystone of the organization's aims and values. (someonetotellitto.org)

Vision

People often get confused by the concepts of mission and vision, but there are some distinct differences. If you can think of your mission statement as the one-liner describing your organization, your vision is your dream for what you want your organization to ultimately affect. It's generally much broader, somewhat longer, and more wide-reaching than your mission. Perhaps you want to feed hungry children in your community. Is your dream to become a model feeding program that others can recreate? Is your dream to end hunger for children in your community completely so that no child goes hungry? Your mission is your goal, and your vision is the complete end game, perhaps after meeting many goals. It's what you're aiming for the world to look like with your organization in it, how you want the world to look as your organization makes an impact. Anything is possible, and it doesn't have to be difficult or complicated. This is simply the tool to get you thinking about the future of your nonprofit and its impact on your community or the world.

If we look at the vision statements as opposed to the mission statements for the organizations I mentioned, look at the differences:

American Red Cross Mission Statement: To prevent and alleviate human suffering in the face of emergencies by mobilizing the power of volunteers and the generosity of donors.

American Red Cross Vision Statement: The American Red Cross, through its strong network of volunteers, donors, and partners, is always there in times of need. We aspire to turn compassion into action so that...

>...all people affected by disaster across the country and around the world receive care, shelter, and hope;

>...our communities are ready and prepared for disasters;

>...everyone in our country has access to safe, lifesaving blood and blood products;

>...all members of our armed services and their families find support and comfort whenever needed; and

...in an emergency, there are always trained individuals nearby, ready to use their Red Cross skills to save lives.

Literacy Council of Northern Virginia Mission Statement: To teach adults the basic skills of reading, writing, speaking, and understanding English so they can access employment and educational opportunities and more fully and equitably participate in the community.

Literacy Council of Northern Virginia Vision Statement: A community empowered by the ability to read, write, speak, and understand English.

M.S. Hershey Foundation Mission Statement: to provide cultural and educational opportunities to the Hershey community.

M.S. Hershey Foundation Vision Statement: The M.S. Hershey Foundation exists to preserve and enhance Milton Hershey's legacy and community vision and to provide education and cultural enrichment to residents and visitors of Hershey, Pennsylvania.

As you can see, mission statements are goal-oriented to give the stakeholders a fast and precise look at what your organization does. Vision statements focus on what your organization aspires to be. Vision statements focus on what the community will look like with your organization in it rather than how your organization will get there.

Have you thought about a potential mission statement for our LALO? If I wrote one, it would probably look something like this: The mission of Lemon Aid for Little Ones is to provide the community with opportunities to support the Child Life Program at Penn State Hershey Children's Hospital through donations to and volunteer support of its lemonade stands locally. This mission statement provides the name of the organization, its goal of supporting the Child Life Program, the ways it's going to do those things, and the offer to the community to become a part of it. It's been found that when you ask for donations as opposed to putting a price on things like cups of lemonade or baked goods, people give more generously. So it was important for us to state that we aren't selling lemonade, so to speak, but we're accepting donations for a cause (the Child Life Program) with a small token in return (the lemonade or cookie or whatever). It's clear, concise, and direct. If the organization grows or changes its goal or programs in the future, the mission statement can be adjusted to reflect that.

As for a vision statement for LALO, it could be written many different ways. We could dream big and envision a world in which children don't get cancer or long-term illnesses and don't have to be hospitalized. While that would be great, since we're not raising money for cancer research or medical interventions, that would not be strongly aligned with our mission. Since we're supporting a program that aims to make sick children as comfortable and happy as possible, we could envision a world where those kids have access to all kinds of creature comforts from home to make their stays the best they possibly could. be. That would be more in line with what we're raising money for, so LALO's vision might be something like: A world in which pediatric patient hospital stays are less frightening and uncomfortable by creating environments that feel more like home.

Should the organization choose to go a different direction, the vision statement could always be changed or finessed as time goes on, but this one relates to what the organization does and how things would look if it's successful.

In addition to mission and vision statements, many organizations also take time to create a list of values by which they will abide. Frequently, organizations post these values on their websites, along with their mission and vision statements, to give the public a well-rounded look at the organization as a whole and how it operates. All of these statements should be developed by a team of people committed to the organization and updated as necessary. Rely on these statements as your foundation. Post them not only on your website but also where you, your employees, your volunteers, and your board members can see them, so everyone is reminded what you are working for. After all, "When you visualize, you materialize." (Denis Waitley)

Motivations and Takeaways

Phew! That was a lot, but you made it. Now you're equipped to really dig into what you want your organization to be and do.

- Collaborate with your potential board members and supporters to develop a succinct but compelling, easy to understand, and memorable mission statement.

- Dream big and write out your vision for what the future of your community or the world will look like with your organization in it.

- Don't get too bogged down or stuck trying to finalize these things. Remember that they can change as the organization changes.

Chapter 6

Getting Legal

Filings and Organizational Documents

Integrity is doing the right thing even when no one is watching.

—C. S. Lewis

Ok, dear reader. We have just tackled a lot of information, so you might want to take time to stand up, stretch, and get a deep breath before we dive in again. Some of this can be very dense, but mastering these first few chapters about creating a firm foundation now will pay you huge dividends in the long run. After all, you are going to be most successful when you focus on being a smart, business-driven organization (for this chapter, that means thorough, organized, and methodical) along with the compassion you have for your cause.

Getting Legal

Perhaps the most daunting task about starting a nonprofit, or any organization for that matter, is the paperwork.

So much paperwork! Yes, there are a lot of forms to complete, blanks to fill in, and documents to submit. But it's actually manageable if you take it one step at a time. And, the more organized and methodical you are, the easier you will make things in the long run.

One benefit of creating a nonprofit organization is that 501(c)(3) organizations are tax- exempt. That means your organization doesn't have to pay federal income taxes or sales tax. These are huge breaks, as these things can add up quickly. All the same, your organization will have to pay other taxes such as property taxes, state and local income taxes, and several other fees.

Before you can become tax-exempt, you must form a corporation. The corporation must be formed because 1) you as a person cannot be a tax-exempt entity, and 2) the organization should be its own entity without your being personally liable for its finances.

Before I explain the process, I want to underscore the absolutely essential need for proper legal counsel when it is necessary. One struggle nonprofits often face is the choice between seeking subject matter expertise and being able to pay for that service. Regardless, there are two areas in which obtaining expert advice is crucial, and those are the areas of legal and accounting services. The reason it's so important to get professional help in these areas is because the laws around these subjects are complex, and the people who can assist you in these areas have had extensive schooling and training. Obtaining that help does not reflect on your own intelligence or capabilities. In fact, it's the smartest thing you can do, unless you yourself are a professional in either of these arenas.

These are areas in which it is dismayingly easy to screw up, and those screwups can have dire ramifications for your organization if not handled properly (think fraud, lawsuits, and even bankruptcy).

Of course, the biggest obstacle to this is cost. The best advice I can give you is to wrap these costs into your startup budget and make sure you will have enough funds to cover them. Going forward, make sure these expenses are budgeted into your cost of operations as non-negotiable budget items. These services will pay for themselves over and over again financially, and the peace of mind you will gain from knowing that your legal and accounting issues are in good hands will be priceless.

Even though you're definitely going to invest in a lawyer and an accountant, you'll still want to know some basics about making your organization a legal entity. As mentioned, the first step is to incorporate your organization so that it can 1) become tax-exempt, and 2) become a legal entity separate from you personally. There are exceptions to incorporation, such as charitable organizations operating with less than $5,000 in annual revenue, but for the majority of cases, incorporating is necessary (your lawyer will make sure you're on the right track). Corporations are governed by state law, and laws and requirements vary from state to state. The best place to find information on your state's process is by searching "incorporating nonprofit corporation in (your state)." That will return results that will tell you which governing agency oversees incorporation in your state. IRS.gov is also helpful in locating state information.

Once you locate where to file your incorporation, you will

need to have the following things ready and available: (note this is not an exhaustive list)

- Name of the organization—this should be the one you want forever!

- The address where you are registering said organization (a real address and not a post office box may be required)

- The names and addresses of any incorporators (see Chapter 7)

- Articles of Incorporation (many states offer forms you can simply complete, although most caution you to consult with a lawyer prior to completing them— on the next page is part of a sample form from the Minnesota Council of Nonprofits)

- The required filing fee (again, this varies by state)

- There will most likely be other items required to be attached to your application, and most states also require a few board members to be named as incorporators on your Articles of Incorporation. Their qualifications might be necessary as well, simply because the state wants to know whether you have a leadership team in place. This is good because it forces you to think about your leadership as soon as possible. Again, each state will have its own requirements.

- Some states will allow applications to be received electronically. That being said, it's extremely important for you to retain not only electronic copies

Template Articles of Incorporation

Electronic template of Articles of Incorporation can be found at www.minnesotanonprofits.org/start-forms-fees.

Amendments to the articles, such as a change in address, change in name or other operational change, must be filed with the Secretary of State. A $55 filing fee applies for each set of amendments.

A copy of the original articles and bylaws should be filed for the organization's records.

The following articles of incorporation are intended only as a model. They show some of the most general ways of writing articles of incorporation. Due to Internal Revenue Service restrictions of tax-exempt organizations, it is necessary for a tax-exempt organization to include some language provided in IRS Publication 557. These statements are noted below. Organizations are free to re-produce all, or parts of the samples provided in this section. Items highlighted in bold type signify information specific to the organization. Other information provided in this sample may or may not fit the needs of a specific organization and should be used only as an example. Organizations should seek the advice of an attorney when drafting important legal documents.

Please note: Sample articles provided by the Secretary of State's Office do not include statements required by the IRS for approval of tax exemptions.

ARTICLES OF INCORPORATION OF **[NONPROFIT ABC]**

The undersigned incorporator is an individual 18 years of age or older and adopt the following articles of incorporation to form a nonprofit corporation (Chapter 317A).

ARTICLE I — NAME

The name of this corporation shall be **[NONPROFIT ABC]**

ARTICLE II — REGISTERED OFFICE ADDRESS

Organizations must include a street address, not a PO Box, as its registered address. It is typically the founder or board president's address, if a permanent office address hasn't yet been determined.

The place in Minnesota where the principal office of the corporation is to be located at **[NONPROFIT ABC'S OFFICE ADDRESS]**

ARTICLE III — PURPOSE

Language provided in Article III is required by the IRS to obtain tax-exempt status. The organization must include this statement and state its charitable purpose, as highlighted in this example. See IRS Publication 557 for details.

This corporation is organized exclusively for charitable, religious and educational as specified in Section 501(c)(3) of the Internal Revenue Code, including for such purposes, the making of distributions to organizations that qualify as exempt organizations under Section 501(c)(3) of the Internal Revenue Code, or the corresponding section of any future federal tax code.

The purpose of this corporation is:
- **to support and conduct non-partisan research, education, and informational activities to increase public awareness of juvenile delinquency;**
- **to combat crime within neighborhoods; and**
- **to prevent community deterioration.**

ARTICLE IV — EXEMPTION REQUIREMENTS

At all times the following shall operate as conditions restricting the operations and activities of the corporation:

Language provided in Article IV is required by the IRS to obtain tax-exempt status. See Publication 557 for more information.

1. No part of the net earnings of the corporation shall inure to the benefit of, or be distributable to its members, trustees, officers or other private persons, except that the corporation shall be authorized and empowered to pay reasonable compensation for services rendered and to make payments and distributions in furtherance of the purpose set forth in the purpose clause hereof.
2. No substantial part of the activities of the corporation shall constitute the carrying on of propaganda or otherwise attempting to influence legislation, or any initiative or referendum before the public, and the corporation shall not participate in, or intervene in (including by publication or distribution of statements), any political campaign on behalf of, or in opposition to, any candidate for public office.

Handbook for Starting a Successful Nonprofit ©

but also paper copies of any important documents for your organization. Keep paper copies in a safe, protected place that you and several others can remember and access. I'm a big fan of three-ring binders and would most likely have an entire bookshelf dedicated to my official documents, policies and procedures manual, and anything else that should be organized and kept where employees and volunteers can find them. In addition, keep a backed-up electronic copy on a portable external drive should you need to access it that way.

- Some states will not actually issue a separate paper certificate of incorporation. Instead, a signature on your application by the state will be considered your incorporation. Additionally, most states require each nonprofit organization to also register with its Bureau of Charitable Organizations or something similar. This registration is a separate requirement if you're going to solicit any type of funds or donations. If your organization operates in multiple states, you will need to apply to solicit charitable donations in each state in which you are conducting business. Bummer, I know.

- Following your application for incorporation, you will also need to apply to the IRS for an Employer Identification Number, or EIN. You will need this number for many reasons, including your application for tax exemption, state and federal reports, and, potentially, for hiring employees. This number remains with your organization forever (it's also a good thing to memorize, as it appears on millions of grant applications, requests for funding, and other documents). This process is free (for a change, yay!) and can be done electronically through the

IRS website. You will need to complete IRS Form SS-4 (search "Form SS-4" in the search box on the IRS website). As IRS forms go, it's a pretty simple one. Again, I refer back to my advice about hiring legal counsel. It's best to make sure someone with a set of legal eyes sees the form before it's submitted. The coolest thing about the EIN number is that if you apply online, you'll get your number right away—woohoo!

The last (and, unfortunately, the most complicated) step in becoming a tax-exempt charitable organization is applying to the IRS for tax exemption. You'll be requesting an IRS determination or ruling that says your organization is indeed a public charity (i.e., it receives at least a third of its revenues from public sources). This requires completion of IRS Form 1023, which will cost you at least $600. It's very long and complicated. Again, I defer to legal counsel despite the fact that the form has step-by-step instructions. Rather comically, your organization may be eligible to complete the shorter 1023 EZ Application, but that's only if the organization expects to make less than $50,000 revenue in the following three years and you can answer no to 26 questions on a seven-page eligibility quiz. Sounds fun and so much easier, right? That's why the best choice is to work with a lawyer to complete these forms accurately and in a timely manner. Then you know for sure that everything will be done properly.

With respect to all of the above requirements, there are some great resources out there that outline additional details and important things to know. The IRS website is a great start, and your state's website will direct you to its section on charities. You can also refer to the back of this book for some great websites and print resources that can be of tremendous help. There is simply no need for either of us to reinvent the wheel.

If we think back to the example of Lemon Aid for Little Ones (LALO), I would complete this process for the state of Pennsylvania. Upon typing "incorporating a nonprofit corporation in Pennsylvania" into my search engine, I find (about halfway through the first page of results) the Department of State website, which directs me to its Business and Charities page. It has links for businesses and for charities (hmmm, perhaps that underscores the problem that nonprofits aren't seen as businesses...). It has additional links for each type of filing that I need to do as well as pdf and Word versions of forms I need. I would carefully comb through the information, making sure I had at least a cursory understanding of what needs to be done. And I would follow that with a consultation with my lawyer to complete the necessary paperwork. I know I'm not proficient enough to complete these steps on my own, and I would feel it would be too risky if I did.

Legal Out There, What About in Here?

Now that you've conquered the big, scary tasks of incorporating, registering, and gaining tax- exempt status, it's time to look inward. You can be excited that you have a legally established organization to move forward with and represent to prospective donors and clients! Yet you need to be ready to do more than just look good. You've got to get your internal structure to match your external appearance, and this is really an area where we can look to the for-profit business playbook.

Have you ever stopped to consider how a house is built? My dad was in construction, so I grew up understanding the ins and outs of home building and can define terms like footers, trusses, and hanging drywall. But even those of you who don't understand construction probably know that you build a strong foundation first. If you're building a two-story home, you certainly can't start with the master bathroom on the second floor and build around it. You've got to start at the bottom, digging the foundation so you have a solid place on which to begin building.

We have to do the same thing with our organizations. We must create a solid foundation on which to build everything else, or else we run the risk of total and complete collapse (think of the Three Little Pigs and the house of straw versus that of bricks). One of those foundational pillars is your mission and vision—what the organization is going to do and how it is going to affect the world. The second is the legal stuff—incorporating, registering, and obtaining tax-exempt status. The third pillar is figuring out how your organization is going to run on the inside and by what process.

At the very heart of running the organization are its bylaws. These are the rules by which your organization operates, including everything from which accounting practices you will use to your hours of operation and your hiring practices. There are different requirements for how thorough bylaws should be from state to state, but there are also some very general bylaws that apply to most organizations. Think of these as your guides—they guide not only the activities of the organization but also the general procedures and procedures that your Board will follow, including how many board members you will have, how long they will serve, and how they'll be elected, because keep in mind, a Board of Directors operates through an electoral process at all times. Decisions are made by vote so that no one person's opinion can steer the organization in a particular direction.

I find bylaws easier to read than articles of incorporation, but they do require more detail and so are often divided into articles, sections, and sub-sections. Just like your mission, your bylaws can be changed as the organization outgrows certain procedures or policies. Changing them will require a voting system that you will lay out within them. In addition, there are no right or wrong ways to complete your bylaws as long as they cover all of the necessary subjects. Your bylaws may look very similar to those of another organization or quite different, as there are a lot of sample bylaws available to help you with the process. A simple Google search can provide a myriad of options on how to lay out your bylaws and what to include. Another great resource is grantspace.org for understanding bylaws and finding samples from other organizations like yours. Your lawyer can also provide you with samples and possibly simple fill-in bylaws.

Bylaws need cleaning and reorganizing, just as a house does every now and again. They might even need a makeover or renovation, so to speak. They should be revisited at least every other year to make sure they are all relevant and continue to be useful. As the organization grows and changes, some rules may need to be adjusted. Consider them an operating manual for your organization. As you hire staff, add volunteers, or create additional programs, your operating manual will need to be updated. Bylaws are not required to be public documents, but allowing the public access to them increases an organization's credibility and transparency and helps build a better relationship with the community and its stakeholders.

In addition to bylaws, it's essential to maintain a proper, up-to-date policies and procedures manual. You can come up with whatever creative name you'd like for this book. It's similar to your bylaws, but is more relevant to your everyday operations and more correlated with your organization's details. It should contain things like personnel policies (behavior, dress code, vacation, sick, and leave time policies), standard operating procedures for your office (security codes, procedures for opening and closing, operating hours, etc.), and explanations of your services and programs. It should contain correct contact information for members of your staff and board (even if you are the only staff member), as well as pertinent vendor information such as your landlord's information, where your equipment came from and who should be called to fix it, and what happens in cases of emergency. It can even include details such as how the phone should be answered, whether messages should be taken via paper or sent to voicemail, and what to promise as far as when someone will get a call back. Nothing is too small to put in writing. Consider that if you need to explain it to someone (an employee, volunteer, board member, or even a consumer), it's a good idea to put it in writing as well.

Your policies and procedures manual should also define proper ways of handling common workplace problems such as conflict resolution and how employees should handle concerns. In one nonprofit I worked for, the policy was that if an employee worked beyond his or her allotted 35 hours a week, those extra hours would be granted as compensation time (comp time) some other day. I was used to this system, as it is very well-accepted in the nonprofit community given that nonprofits can rarely afford to pay overtime. So, I took my comp time during weeks when I had little work to do, or if I wanted extra time off for a trip. Keep in mind that my assigned work was always completed well and thoroughly, and I gave my co-worker and director (there were only three of us total) proper notice (I never just called in to take the day off or left early without letting others know at the beginning of the workweek).

The only catch is that I worked alongside another woman who was older than I was and slightly less computer literate. Therefore, I was able to accomplish my workload much faster than she could. One day, I got called into the director's office and told that "some people are upset you're taking your comp time." Now, first of all, with only two of us in the office, I knew exactly who "some people" were. Secondly, I was entitled to this time, as the director was admitting, but my co-worker was upset that I actually took it as opposed to just letting it accrue and not using it. It was a written company policy that I could take my comp time, but apparently there were unwritten and unspoken rules that it should only be taken at certain times and with everyone's approval.

There are several things wrong with this scenario. If a policy is written, it needs to be enforced whether others like it or not. Furthermore, it was none of my co-worker's business when I was taking my time as long as my work was complete.

Finally, this was a situation of sheer cattiness that should never have been mentioned to me in the first place as that was unfair and unprofessional of the director. She should have shut down my co-worker's complaint immediately. This, combined with several other things, ultimately led to my leaving the organization.

Your policy and procedures manual should be kept readily available to all employees in an area that's easily accessible, like at a front desk or in a conference room. It should be also be offered to potential new hires at the interview process so they can decide whether they can abide by your rules. Finally, it should be required reading, with acknowledgement of its receipt for all new staff members and volunteers, so everyone begins on the same page. It should also be amended as necessary. This is the way for-profit businesses run, and it should be the way you run your organization as well.

Motivations and Takeaways

- Get a lawyer!
- 1) Incorporate
  2) Register
  3) Apply for EIN
  4) Apply for tax-exemption
- Build your bylaws
- Create your Policies and Procedures Manual
- Don't reinvent the wheel. It's all out there—find what applies to you!

CHAPTER 7

Who's Leading Who?
Your Board of Directors

*If your actions inspire others to dream more, learn
more, do more and become more, you are a leader.*
—JOHN QUINCY ADAMS

By making it to this point, you've already covered some of the most laborious details. Now we can talk about broader and more interesting stuff, like who's going to accompany you on this journey and what you're actually going to do together. Think of your people: employees, volunteers, and board members, as the fourth pillar of that house we talked about building a solid foundation for in Chapter 6. Figuring out who those people are and what they are going to do is much more fun than paperwork and acronyms!

Who Is the Board of Directors,
and What the Heck Do They Do?

Although it's tempting, especially for an introverted,

type-A person like me, to take an idea and run with it solo (because after all, it was your idea and you want to make the decisions, right?), one key component to creating a nonprofit is building a successful Board of Directors. In the nonprofit industry, Boards of Directors (boards) are not only a legally required group of people for the governance of your organization but also an integral element in fulfilling the mission you've set forth (and a mission in which they have hopefully had input).

Boards have multiple responsibilities, the primary one being fiduciary—upholding the public's trust in the organization. Because nonprofits don't have owners in the way that for-profit businesses do, boards oversee the organizations in the ways that owners would, including things such as being listed as incorporators of the organization on its application for incorporation. Since nonprofits are created for public benefit, the primary responsibility of the board is to make sure that the organization is indeed benefiting the public while not abusing its rights and privileges, such as being tax-exempt. In other words, boards make sure that organizations aren't just paying lip service to their missions and skimming money behind the scenes.

Boards of directors are responsible for financial oversight of the organization and supervising you, as its leader, with whatever title you choose to take (manager, director, founder, Executive Director, etc.), so pick your board carefully! Boards also make broad, strategic decisions like whether it's prudent to expand programs, rather than daily decisions like which brand of copy paper to use. Board members are required to put the organization's welfare above other interests when making decisions for the organization, and they must act in accordance with the organization's bylaws. In addition, nonprofit board members are almost never compensated for their service and cannot personally benefit from any funds the organization earns. Members may be reimbursed for expenses, however. Boards also have the secondary responsibilities of strategic planning, hiring leadership, and, most times, fundraising.

This is all sounding complicated, so why must it be done this way? Well, the primary reason is to ensure that your organization is operating in a legally and financially sound way, doing business honestly, and fulfilling your mission. Just as importantly, collaboration and teamwork are indispensable for making the right decisions for the organization. Although at times it can seem unwieldy to take into consideration the opinions of multiple people, it's also during those times when we're exposed to new ideas and perspectives we might not have considered. When you build a talented, diverse panel of people to oversee your organization, you'll be in the best position to receive honest feedback, diverse viewpoints, and angles on subjects you hadn't considered. Since everyone brings his or her own specialty and wealth of knowledge to your table, you'll expose yourself to resources you never knew you had, and give yourself the help of many brains to tackle problems that seem overwhelming. You will also likely get some great donors and volunteers from the board you create.

Creating a Board

Even though nonprofit and for-profit businesses alike have boards of directors, recruiting people for a board is not an easy task. Ideally, you're looking for people who have passion for your mission, will be strong advocates for your programs, and will be honest, professional representatives of your organization. Since these board members are responsible for the fiscal health of your organization, they are also the ones who can potentially be legally responsible for its debts should it not survive. You need people who will not only put themselves on the line but also provide ethical oversight to your organization, be willing to donate generously, and sweep a floor or stuff envelopes when necessary. It's a tall order to fill.

A successful, working board was a particular challenge for former Executive Director (ED) Patti Donnelly of the Literacy Council of Northern Virginia. When she took the ED position, she faced an organization that had a strong outward reputation but also had overworked employees and an infrastructure that was crumbling. She also faced a very kind but somewhat unaware and disconnected board. Of the nine members, five were elected as "program representatives," which meant they'd volunteered successfully for one of the organization's several programs and were subsequently chosen to serve on the board. They were well-meaning individuals who had a lot to say about how the programs should be managed, but they were not visionary leaders or experienced at running a business, nor were they familiar with fundraising or strategic planning

As often happens when a board is inherited rather than chosen, they were also very resistant to change. As Patti explained, "There were four who had some business sense or professional experience outside of education, but only one had prior board service experience. Plus, like the lack of management systems in place, the bylaws were inadequate on defining term limits, board recruitment, and on-boarding. It is challenging to address changing the structure of the board and suggesting defining roles and practices, when these people are your boss. It took a full 10 years to get a fully-functioning board." When Patti left LCNV in September of 2017, the 14-person board was running smoothly, due to the diligence she put into building a strong, knowledgeable, process- oriented board, which included recruiting new members and replacing others.

Building a successful board like Patti's can be difficult but doable, particularly when you're starting from scratch and not having to change long-standing traditions. The first thing to keep in mind is that you want to find people who are enthusiastic and committed to the mission you've set forth. If your organization is going to feed children after school, a board member most interested in donating to art museums is not your ideal board member. You also want board members who are part of the community in which you serve. Though it's always helpful to gain some outside perspective, board members who have a personal stake in your town or region will be most interested in something benefiting that area. Additionally, you want to find board members who are academically and ethnically diverse so that you have some content experts to rely on and diverse cultural experiences to take into consideration.

The size of the board can vary from organization to organization and time to time. Most startup organizations begin with smaller boards in the range of 5–8 people until they are able to build relationships and encourage additional stakeholders to join the board. There are benefits and challenges to both small and larger boards, and it is by no means a one-size-fits-all proposition. Small boards are more limited in their knowledge, experience, and fundraising abilities, whereas larger boards can be difficult to pin down for meetings or make decisions quickly. In addition, the size of your board may vary through the lifetime of the organization. The most important thing to keep in mind is how actively engaged you want your board members to be. Do not feel as though you need to bring on additional board members simply because you have a small board. Bring on people who have a passion for your mission and the willingness to help in multiple capacities, including directing you to potential funding sources.

Where are you going to find these amazing, talented, visionary leaders with a mind for business and a heart for your mission? The best way to find them is to network. Networking can seem daunting, but it doesn't have to be overwhelming. Really, networking is just a fancy word for going out and talking to people. Start by talking to people you know and sharing your mission and vision. If those people don't have the knowledge, enthusiasm, or resources you need, don't be afraid to ask them if they know someone else who might be of help to you.

If E. and I wanted to follow through in making LALO (our lemonade stand) a full-fledged nonprofit organization, we would want to recruit a small board as well. As it was, I didn't need to recruit board members, but I did need to network a bit to find out how E. could best donate her proceeds. She was eager to help kids with cancer because she had learned at school about the Children's Miracle Network

THONs and dance-a-thons college students were having to raise money for Children's Miracle Network hospitals, one of which is in our town. The local elementary and high school students started having these dance fundraisers too, and the elementary kids learned that the money was going to help sick children. Since this made an impact on E., I had to find the best place to donate the money she made.

I approached a friend of mine from high school whose sister works at our local children's hospital. Through my friend, I got in touch with her sister, Sarah, and was able to learn about areas in which the money could go directly to help the children. She explained that E.'s donation could go directly as cash to the Child Life Program that provides kids in the hospital with toys, games, activities, and things to make it feel more like home, or that we could use our money to go out and buy some of the things on the Child Life Program's wish list. Of course, for my young daughter, it was much more fun and made a bigger impact on her to go shopping for things kids like her would want. So, we delivered a cart's worth of games, toys, and toiletries to our friend in Child Life.

In our case, it wasn't difficult to find someone who knew what we needed, and with our interconnectedness as a society today, it's much easier than in the past to find someone who has the knowledge you need. If we did indeed need to form a board, I probably would have started by asking Sarah to join since she has direct contact with others who work with sick children. Sarah might also have recommendations for potential board members who have access to the right people and resources we would need. Had I not known my friend, I may have cold-called the local hospital, started asking other friends (maybe any nurses or doctors I knew), or even put a call out on social media to see if anyone knew someone who worked at the Children's Hospital who might be able to help me. Just sharing with others what you're aiming for is the easiest and best way to go whether you're looking for somewhere to donate, some knowledge you don't have, or board members who will commit to your organization.

Once you have some names and ideas, the best way to recruit people is through personal invitation. Though it might seem stressful to pick up the phone and call someone you've never spoken to before, this is the best way to start. Whether you are able to speak to someone or have to leave a voicemail, always follow up with an email to introduce (or reintroduce) yourself and reiterate the important points of the call. If you don't get a return email or phone call, follow up in one week. Ask for 30 minutes of someone's time to get a cup of coffee and explain your mission and goals. Don't be afraid to ask if the person knows anyone else who might be interested in supporting your organization in one way or another.

Another great way to search for potential board members is to think in categories. If we think about LALO, what groups of people can you think of who would have a stake in wanting to help sick children? Well, parents for sure, although probably not those of currently ill, hospitalized children, as they most likely are dealing with too much themselves. However, parents who have had their children treated, or know someone who has, may wish to give back by volunteering in some way (we'll cover volunteers in a future chapter). Who else might be willing to support this organization?

It might seem like your cause is an easy "sell" like this

one—after all, most people want children to be well and free from suffering or at the very least as happy as they can be in the hospital—but that doesn't mean everyone has the time or the inclination to get directly involved. For LALO, we might want to look in places like local churches and businesses who may either be looking for a philanthropic project or have access to larger amounts of funds. Libraries and after- school organizations might be interested in making donations or supporting the program in another way. Even major local and national employers of the parents of the sick children might have an interest in the program, considering parents of ill children need extra time off and extra support. If those employers can help either the children themselves or advance the science to help keep children healthy, it benefits them by keeping their parents working and their bottom lines growing. As the organization grows, we could even approach restaurant owners or food service suppliers who might be interested in donating the lemonade itself so that most of our donations could go directly to the children as opposed to supplies. Any of these groups of people could have resources to offer, whether they be donations, volunteers, or board members. And if they don't, chances are they will know someone who would be.

A note of caution. As you're looking for board members and actively recruiting them, keep in mind that it should be a two-sided interview process. Yes, you're looking for people to help you, but you don't want to choose the wrong people either. Just because someone might be willing doesn't mean they're the best fit. It's tempting to simply fill a board with any warm bodies that are available, but that does nothing to help your organization. Be discerning in choosing people who you not only like but who can also provide you with significant benefit for the organization, whether that be access to potential funding, expert knowledge, or business savviness.

Who Else Should Serve on the Board?

As I mentioned, it can be very tempting to load your board with family, friends, and paid staff members (because your heart feels inclined to do so). But I don't recommend it (that would not be using your head). A board packed with family members would be a very biased board, and it would not provide you with the diversity of skills, experiences, talents, and even funds that you need. For those reasons, that would never fly in the for-profit world. In addition, you'd be missing the opportunity to connect with new donors who would support your mission. Finally, family members and friends can easily become victims of groupthink.

Groupthink is a psychological concept that tells us that a group of well-intentioned people can make irrational or non-optimal decisions due to their urge to conform or the pressure from others not to dissent.[7] In other words, groupthink happens when a group of well-meaning people try to make good decisions in a group, but whose desire to fit in with the others or keep the peace overwhelms their abilities to make decisions for the best outcome. I don't know about you, but it's much more difficult for me to say no to a bad idea when I'm surrounded by a group of family or friends as opposed to when I'm surrounded by those with whom I have no personal relationship.

As for staff, it's important to keep paid staff members and the board of directors separate so that conflicts of interest don't occur. Conflicts of interest can come up when people have loyalties to separate entities. For example, if staff members would like a raise and they also sit on the board, the body that votes on and approves or denies the raises, there's a clear conflict of interest. There are other decisions that might affect staff members that the board has the responsibility to make, including reorganizing programs, having to cut expenses, or rearranging the organizational structure. These could easily become highly emotional decisions if staff members are also board members. Therefore it is much less messy and much more prudent to separate the two.

There are exceptions to the rule, especially with respect to founders of startup organizations. Founders like you often become staff members, particularly leaders of their organizations such as Executive Directors, who also sit on their boards because they began the vision and passion to form the nonprofit in the first place. You want to be integral and informed on how the organization develops. The best way to handle this is for you as the founder to be a member of the board who cannot hold an elected position or, in the very least, not hold the role of board chairperson/president. Therefore, you are running and managing the organization, making day-to-day decisions, but you also have the board to help you develop the vision for the organization. Since the board serves as your boss as the Executive Director, it would be a conflict of interest for you to serve as the chairperson for the group of people who oversee you.

Should you choose, as the founder, to take on the role of

Executive Director but not desire to sit on the board, that is also a possibility. Keep in mind that, as the Executive Director, you will probably have to attend most board meetings, but you would not have to take on additional duties. On the flip side, you would not be able to vote on any matters the board is deciding.

For LALO, E. would be the founder of the organization. She might also decide to be the manager or Executive Director (ok, so maybe in about a decade or so …). Therefore, we would form a board, and she could sit on it and help direct the organization with input, but nothing would be solely left up to her. As with all wide-reaching, organizational matters, the board would have the final decision via vote as laid out in the bylaws. I could also serve on the board unless I wanted to become a staff member of hers. In contrast, she could also remain the founder and not run the organization. Since she's a minor, she could be the founder of the organization, and we could form a board and hire a staff to run with her idea. She could always remain the founder in title, as could you.

How Should the Board Operate?

How does a board run? There are many ways and styles of handling the management of the board. It's a delicate dance between the management (usually the executive director) and the board, a give-and-take, a cooperative push and pull. The leadership of the organization is shared by the executive director and the board. The executive director must be prepared to give a report at each board meeting, sharing the highlights and challenges of the day-to-day business of the organization. The board members must be willing to listen, offer suggestions, and vote on matters of overall goals and policies on which the staff must be willing to act. Therefore, the executive director also acts as a liaison between the staff and board, advocating for her staff when necessary and explaining what it's like to provide the day-to-day service. Board members may not beaware of how physically or emotionally taxing the daily work may be, and they may not understand the best ways to deliver the service. Even so, they can be tremendous assets who can provide resources, information, and policies that will help instead of hurting the staff.

Patti Donnelly dealt with this push and pull at the Literacy Council of Northern Virginia. Lines between staff and board duties became blurred when one board member insisted on trying to manage staff members herself. She was a very dedicated board member who wanted the organization's annual fundraiser to succeed, but she went about it the wrong way. She tried to assign staff members particular tasks when her job as a board member in this case was to oversee the event more generally, assist in recruiting attendees, and lead the fundraising efforts. It was Patti's job as the Executive Director to decide which staff members were responsible for which tasks. In other words, board members should not be going directly to staff members to try and manage daily operations. Still, they should receive monthly financial statements from the ED that they should be proficient in understanding. Board members should be able to explain, line by line, the status of the operational budget each month.

As for the actual procedures of running a board and/or a board meeting, most boards choose to govern themselves by Robert's Rules of Order. These are a set of parliamentary procedures businesses can use to conduct meetings, vote on changes, and run efficiently. You may be familiar with many of these procedures such as making a motion, seconding a motion, and voting on a matter. How your board will run meetings may be laid out in your bylaws. For resources on Robert's Rules of Order and other board-related topics, visit boardsource.org.

Avoiding Common Pitfalls

Building and maintaining a board of directors can be tricky. There are a lot of balls to juggle, and if you're not careful, they can start flying out of control. So here's my best advice at avoiding some of the most common pitfalls.

One easy way to avoid reusing stale ideas and to keep things fresh is to continually update your board of directors. Now, continually doesn't mean every few weeks or months. Continually, in this case, means every year to two or three years. Setting term limits on board members not only helps rotate in new blood but also keeps the relationships from becoming stagnant. It doesn't allow for cliques to be formed among members, and it aids in member recruitment because potential members know their time commitment will be limited. Board limits can vary from two to three years, and it's best to stagger terms among board members so that not everyone completes their terms of service at the same time. It would be extremely challenging and perhaps defeating to have to retrain an entirely new board all at once.

Patti Donnelly of the Literacy Council of Northern

Virginia developed several strategies to assist with board recruitment and retention, which can both be difficult. When a member of the board was getting ready to complete their service, Patti asked them to find a proper replacement. This worked well because board members were well-connected, familiar with the commitment to the organization and its needs, and subsequently felt a sense of responsibility to provide a beneficial replacement. This took pressure off of Patti and other board members to constantly recruit new people, and the links that board members had to new board members allowed for smooth transitions.

Another challenge, once you have established a board, is retaining those board members. Remember, being a board member is a volunteer job, so people are not required, so to speak, to fulfill their commitments. They must be motivated to do so. One way Patti was able to retain board members for the entire length of their terms was to create strong peer-to-peer relationships among the board members. In other words, when people are friends and like each other, they want to come to meetings, as opposed to feeling like it's a chore to attend. By having board members recruit their own professional friends and people they had respect for in the business world, Patti was able to craft an environment in which her board members liked to come to meetings because they knew they would see people they wanted to see.

Building strong collegial relationships among board members was also key to attendance at yearly board retreats. When it came time to gather the board for a designated time to focus on the future of the organization, Patti was able to get perfect attendance for three years in a row once the organization began holding it at one of the board member's places of business. A board member got his company to donate a beautiful conference space for the retreat, and because all of the board members had respect for each other and no one wanted anyone else to look bad, every board member showed up. Having those retreats at a fellow board member's company was a huge asset. Not only did people want the host to look good, but the board was also treated to a different professional atmosphere, and the host felt proud to show off his company.

How you court and recruit members is as important as what you do to retain them. We spoke of how to find them, but what happens once you find a suitable person? You should be very upfront and clear with that person about the expected duties, responsibilities, and time commitment. Don't shy away from sharing how much time your organization might require because you need people who are willing to devote the necessary time. Making sure potential (and current) members know what's expected of them is more than half the battle. The best way to do this is to have documents explaining what is expected. Duties and responsibilities should be laid out clearly and concisely and provided to a prospective member once you have chosen to offer them a position on the board.

Offering someone a position on the board is an important decision. Remember that you need to make sure you have taken the time to vet the person to be the best of your ability. Familiarize yourself with their experience, skills, and personality, as these are all very important considerations. When you're first starting out and don't have a board yet to meet, you might want to invite potential board members out for coffee, to your office space if you have one, or to an event you may be attending on behalf of your organization. You may also want to set up a meeting between potential board members to see how well they get along. Instead of a formal board meeting, that could be a brainstorming session or an introduction to the organization in which you ask for their feedback.

Once you have a more established organization with a board that meets regularly, inviting (or requiring) potential board members to attend a board meeting before offering them a position is a good move. This allows someone to get to know your organization and process and allows current board members to make an informed decision about bringing him/her on. Be very clear about not offering a position before the other board members have approved the decision, as board members are one of the items that the board of directors usually votes on. Once a person is offered a position, they should be oriented to all of your policies and procedures. Provide them with a Board Member Orientation Packet that includes:

- Materials about your organization, including marketing materials and descriptions of programs and services (maybe you've developed a brochure or even a one-page explanation of who you are and what you do)
- Past board meeting minutes (if you have them)
- Copies of your articles of incorporation and bylaws
- Conflict of interest and confidentiality policies
- Copies of financial statements
- Calendar(s) of events and meetings
- Board member roster (if you have one yet)
- Any other pertinent information

This is the best way to make sure your new board member has a full, clear picture of the organization. They can then follow up with questions to you or other board members as necessary. If you don't have a board yet, you might want to provide potential members with some personal references, people who could vouch for your work ethic, dedication to your cause, and ability to begin your organization. In addition, you'll want to ask your board members to sign a board contract. This will ensure that they've been apprised of the required responsibilities and expectations. This should be signed both by the new board member as well as the founder or the board president.

This brings me to an additional point. You and your board have the ability to decide how you want to structure yourselves—what types of officers and terms of service you want to use. Some states have laws requiring certain officers to be in place, so be sure to check those first. The most common structure includes a president or chairperson, vice president, secretary, and treasurer. The most important thing to remember is that each officer's roles and responsibilities are spelled out ahead of time. In addition, as your board grows, you may need to form committees for certain projects or to oversee larger areas of operation such as finance, development, and programming. In general, most people do not like additional committee work, so be sure whatever committees you choose to form are for a specific reason, require a very concrete time commitment, and disband should they complete their task or become irrelevant or ineffective.

Another common pitfall with boards of directors is holding inefficient and ineffective meetings. Make sure you or your board president creates a cohesive agenda complete with allotted times for each topic that is distributed ahead of time to allow others to prepare for the meeting. The president or chairperson should stick as strictly as possible to the agenda, and a secretary or volunteer should keep accurate meeting minutes. Do not allow certain members to belabor points that have already been decided. Occasionally you will have someone try to hijack the meeting with their own ideas and agendas. If that continues, the person may need to be asked to leave the board. On the other hand, if it is a one-time thing, the president or chairperson can gently steer the person back to the agenda. Don't add things to the agenda during the meeting if that can be helped, and stick to the time periods you allot on the agenda. Work out a meeting schedule that works for you and the board members—meeting too often will deter people, but you must make sure you meet often enough to conduct business. The meeting schedule should be outlined in your bylaws. It's possible to hold meetings virtually as well (Skype, Zoom, etc.), but keep in mind that a lot of relationship building and networking between board members cannot happen virtually. Therefore, you'll want to hold at least a couple of board meetings a year in person. Be sure to engage board members in between meetings, whether by email, phone calls, or group text messages. The more engaged you keep them, the more interested they will stay.

Since the board is responsible for the financial health and management of the organization, one way to help ensure proper procedures and smart money management is for the board to create a policy on how much money the Executive Director can spend without its approval. This may seem like overkill, but it helps keep expenditures in check and helps maintain a system of checks and balances. Perhaps the ED can spend no more than $1,500 at a time without the board's approval. Of course, this depends on the size of the organization and its budget, but that amount can always be increased over time. This allows the ED some flexibility in spending when something breaks (the printer, the copier, a computer) or when staff need something (additional program supplies, a small reward, etc.). It still precludes the ED from making any major financial decisions without board approval. This helps the organization stay solvent and maintains a system of checks and balances.

Speaking of finances, because you can't financially compensate your board members, the best ways to keep them engaged with the work of the organization are to not only have expectations and responsibilities spelled out but also to express your appreciation regularly. Simple, verbal thank-yous and written notes of appreciation can mean a lot, particularly when a board member has gone out of their way to be helpful. Small gifts of appreciation recognizing years of service or holidays are greatly appreciated. In addition, share progress and feel-good stories so they feel connected to the impact the organization is making on its clients. Mention board members repeatedly in newsletters and media, and show your gratitude.

Motivations and Takeaways

Who knew having a board of directors could be so perplexing!

- Consider your board of directors as owners of the organization, responsible for keeping the organization honest, fiscally sound, legal, and on track.

- Recruit board members who are committed to your mission, willing to give of their time and financial resources, and provide necessary skills to further your mission.

- Talk to people to find potential board members and avoid loading your board with family, friends, and staff members.

- Set up expectations, responsibilities, and board orientation packets ahead of time. Make sure everyone is clear on their roles by having them sign a contract saying they've received the information.

- Run meetings efficiently and effectively.

- Firmly encourage the board to set a spending limit without the board's approval for the manager or Executive Director.

- Appreciate your board!

Chapter 8

Show Me the Money!

Fundraising and Grant Writing

I have tried raising money by asking for it,
and by not asking for it.
I always got more by asking for it.

—Millard Fuller

The biggest challenge facing any nonprofit is raising money. This concern begins almost the second you have an idea. You want to feed children? Where are you getting the funds? You want to teach people how to read? How are you going to pay for materials and teachers? You want to help children in the hospital? With what money?

Fundraising can be a tremendously overwhelming task. There are a lot of ways to go about it, and there are plenty of ways to be successful at it. It can also be a bit confusing because the for-profit sector provides a product or a service for a price, and that's how it makes money. The nonprofit sector, on the

95

other hand, provides human service products that usually aren't paid for by the client or the person receiving the service. Therefore, the funding for those services must be provided by someone else, namely donors. Since that money is provided by donors, nonprofits also have the responsibility to spend that money wisely in working toward their missions.

Making Money Like a For-Profit

Even though your organization will rely on fundraising to survive, your organization is also responsible for bringing in some of its own revenue, or making money, just like any business in the for-profit world. That may sound confusing because it implies you have to be selling a good or service— and you are! Since not all of your clients will pay for your services though, you have to be creative about coming up with other ways to bring in money, in addition to fundraising.

Executive Director of The M.S. Hershey Foundation Donald Papson and his team have to develop multiple ways to increase revenue to support the arts in Hershey, Pennsylvania. The Foundation was established and funded by Milton Hershey in 1935 to provide educational and cultural benefits for the community's residents and visitors. These include The Hershey Story Museum, the Hershey Theatre, the Hershey Gardens, and the Hershey Community Archives. People pay to enter the Museum and the Gardens and buy tickets to events at the Theater. But those sources of income do not nearly cover the costs of the Foundation. Therefore, the Foundation not only fundraises but also finds other ways to make money. For example, the Foundation developed a tribute tree and bench program in which people can purchase the right to name a tree or a bench in the Gardens after a loved one. This type of creative program requires very little additional effort on the part of the Foundation but brings in extra income.

In addition to finding creative (but always legal!) ways of bringing in income, you also have to be smart with your money. This is where it pays to really think like a for-profit business. You have to learn when to spend and when to save. For-profit businesses are always looking for smart investments, and one of the smartest investments you can make is in your people: your employees, your volunteers, and your board members. Although this costs money, it's one of the very best places to invest because good people will bring success to your organization. Even though nonprofits often have a difficult time paying market rates for hourly and salaried positions, there are times when you will absolutely need to do so in order to bring the smartest, hardest-working, most talented people to your organization. Keep in mind that you're competing not only against other nonprofits but also for-profit businesses who are looking to hire the best.

There are a few ways organizations deal with this challenge. Sometimes they weigh the costs of changes versus the benefits and end up restructuring their employees when necessary (we'll talk about independent contractors versus employees in the next chapter). Sometimes they can find cheaper labor when it's appropriate and available. It would not be prudent to hire a "cheap" accountant or program specialist, but it might be worthwhile to look into internship programs and service programs like AmeriCorps. Many young adults use programs like AmeriCorps to do a year of service in areas across the country for a small stipend. Students in college and graduate school are often looking for internships, both paid and unpaid, to gain experience. It also pays to make smart use of volunteers. Volunteers can do many tasks and serve in many roles that can save employees time and effort. You simply need to find the right fit for the volunteer. As you grow, it will also be worthwhile to invest some of your organization's money. A good accountant can point you in the direction of a good financial advisor.

Getting Started

There are multiple potential funding sources for nonprofits. The first and largest portion of private (not governmental) money given to nonprofits is from individuals. In other words, chances are that the majority of your funds will, at least initially, come from individual contributions. Individual contributions can come in many forms. Individuals can donate at any time but can also make special contributions like annual gifts (given once a year), major gifts (a large amount of money with respect to your budget), or planned gifts or bequests (donations made through wills after someone dies).

Some nonprofits solicit donations by offering memberships in which people can pay to belong to the organization and get certain benefits in return. Some nonprofits even use crowdfunding platforms (think Kickstarter, Indiegogo, GoFundMe, etc.), especially as they are getting off the ground. Many nonprofits use a special event as a fundraiser in which people pay to participate or attend. These are often successful, but the amount of money you expect to bring in must far exceed the cost of the event in order for it to be worthwhile. Nonprofits also receive contributions from businesses (corporate contributions), which can come in the form of cash or donated goods. Finally, most nonprofits also apply for grants, whether through governmental agencies or private foundations. Every nonprofit uses some combination of all of these funding sources to be successful.

We covered briefly the idea of startup funding and creating a startup budget. That money, or seed money, is how you are going to start your organization. People choose to do this in many different ways, although it can be difficult to find grants or solicit corporate donations when you are just starting out. Some founders contribute their own seed money. Many people begin with who they know and start by asking friends and family for donations. Any of these can be successful depending on your mission and your connections. What remains constant is that integral to this process is the trust that your potential donors or funders must have in you to start your organization. If you have a proven track record of reliability, dependability, and honesty, people who support you are going to have confidence in your idea and ability to execute it. If, on the other hand, you have difficulty fulfilling commitments, finishing projects, or following through on accomplishing things, your potential donors may not be eager to support your idea. They must feel like you are going to be an honest and trustworthy steward of their donations, using them as you promised you would in a responsible and meaningful way.

Whether you are looking for startup money or the funds to continue your mission, this is another area in which a plan is integral to your success. Going about finding funding is best done systematically in a pre-planned, orderly way. This is one area in which it is of utmost importance to not be haphazard or random in your approach. For example, if you contact someone about a donation but don't have a plan or a way of keeping track of who's asking who, a volunteer or employee of yours could also approach the same person, confusing them and making them think you are disorganized. People generally don't want to give to organizations that are disorganized or chaotic. They don't want to provide their well-earned money to an organization in which it appears that the right hand doesn't know what the left hand is doing.

Making such a plan does not require specific formatting or complicated documents. The best way to begin is simply by brainstorming who you know, who you would like to know, and who you think would donate. These can be friends, family, acquaintances, etc. You can even put people on this list who you would like to meet or obtain a donation from. With brainstorming, nothing is off limits. Once you have a list, quantify your fundraising goals. You need to be ambitious but also realistic when thinking about what you want to raise versus what you are likely to raise.

Next, you must think about how you're going to describe your organization and your goals in a way that interests people. Creating this branding or messaging is very important. You want to communicate your cause, prove that you can fulfill a need, and possibly elicit a strong emotional reaction to get people engaged. Think about what you can offer donors versus what they can offer you. Is your organization one of a kind? Is your cause urgent? How far do your services reach?

Are you as the founder well-known or do you have someone on your team who is? Anything that can make you unique and help convince people that your organization is the right one to donate to in order to get the job done is what you need to communicate. It's also hugely important that this message is consistent across your entire organization. Make sure every employee, volunteer, and board member is telling possible donors the same message.

Once you have a startup budget of what you will need, a goal of what you will raise, and a clear idea of what your message will be, decide who you will approach from your list. Do some additional research as well. You can use donor lists from other organizations and advice from others. You can become good friends with your preferred search engine and scour the internet. In addition, be vigilant about what's going on in your community. Research is your friend in getting to know as much as possible about your potential donors. Read the local news, stay up-to-date on community events, and pay attention to things like donor name displays, programs from events, public television and radio credits, and other organizations' annual reports. There are loads of potential donors everywhere! Given that, your next step is to divide up the work. I realize at the beginning you will be doing most of the work, but as soon as you can recruit some help, you should do so. It's perfectly ok for the first people that help you to be volunteers. That's how many organizations get started. Just be sure to pick the right ones (more on that in Chapter 9).

In preparing to approach potential donors, you will also want to develop some sort of one- page information sheet that you will be able to leave with people after you make a request. Remember your elevator pitch? Well, this is like an elevator pitch for fundraising on paper. This should be short enough that people will actually read the entire thing, but should include things like your contact information and website; your mission; the services you offer; the community need you are addressing; any quotes, testimonials, or photos you have from people you have served and the giving opportunities you have.

For LALO, for example, we would include our mission, what we do, how much money we're aiming to raise, and something to grab the donor's attention like, "A donation of $25 will allow us to purchase three items to make a child's hospital stay more comfortable." Any time you can tie a certain amount of money to a specific outcome, do it. People are much more likely to donate when they can visualize what their donation is actually going to do. You can also offer donors incentives for their donations such as a free t-shirt or trinket or their name recognized in your organization's written materials. Keep in mind that before recognizing a donor publicly, you should obtain their permission.

When you have your materials prepared, it's time to approach people personally. Face-to-face is always the best way to ask for support. When that can't be accomplished, a phone call is possible. One of the most important things to remember is that after each interaction with a potential donor, it is imperative to follow up with a thank you note or email. Gratitude goes a long way in developing relationships with donors, as does minding your manners.

When you approach someone for a donation, break the ice with a very brief conversation about something you have in common to begin to build rapport. But don't waste a donor's time either. Succinctly provide how you got involved or founded the organization, why, and what it does. Be firm and positive, but not pushy. You may make your ask in that very first meeting or you may choose to use that meeting to promote an upcoming giving campaign or program. Keep in mind that not all potential donors will have the ability to give, and recognize when a donor is not in the position to contribute or may feel uncomfortable. In all cases, thank them for their time and provide them with your one-page information sheet and your contact information. I encourage you to follow up with each person via email to, at the very least, thank them for their time as well as their support.

There are many other ways to raise individual donations. Some larger organizations use direct mail. You may want to try a letter-writing campaign. You might also want to do some online fundraising, including collecting email addresses, and soliciting donations that way. You should also consider providing a platform for donations through your website. As you grow, you will want to take advantage of many different ways to solicit individual donations.

Special Events

One way many organizations obtain individual donations is through special fundraising events. This subject alone could be its own book or at least its own chapter, but I want to give you an overview with a few simple points.

Lots of organizations hold fundraising events. If you want to do so, make sure yours is unique or engaging enough that you will have an audience. Chances are, you're competing for your audience's time with many other events like 5ks, silent auctions, and speakers, among other things. Keep the cost of your event reasonable. If you want to ask someone to speak at your event, but the costs of the speaker and the venue and the refreshments are going to potentially exceed what you hope to make from the event, rethink things. You must be in a good position to actually make money off of a special fund-raising event.

Make sure that your target audience understands that the event is for fundraising. People are often very generous and giving when it comes to events like these, but they must know ahead of time that the purpose of the event is to raise money, not to simply enjoy themselves. If they know this, they will likely come prepared with their checkbooks. They won't do so if you don't publicize your event properly.

Start small. These events can be costly and very time-consuming to plan and execute. When you're ready to step into the special events arena, begin small and conservatively. Try to obtain a venue and refreshments for free and make the activity or entertainment cost-effective. Ideas like big-name speakers should be reserved for events where you stand to make a substantial amount of money—think a third or more of your annual budget.

Ask for sponsorships and donations early. There are so many nonprofits out there asking for money that you need to ask early and often. Pay attention to the fiscal years that corporations and businesses use, and always ask for sponsorship money or donations as close to the beginning of that business's fiscal year as possible. This gives the best chance of obtaining funding because as the year goes on and large for-profits pass out funding to other organizations, your chances of receiving money decrease significantly. Follow each business's guidelines for requesting funds or in-kind (product) donations. In addition, follow up when you haven't gotten an answer and always be sure to credit your donors and sponsors at the event as well as via thank you notes, whether mailed or emailed.

Keep in mind that special fundraising events are reliant heavily on well-planned and well- executed details. The difference between a 'nice' event that raises a little money and a 'great' event is all in the small things—how you invite attendees and greet them, how your refreshments are displayed, how much seating is available, how loud any background music is. Triple check all printed material for mistakes in spelling, grammar, and titles of guests. Make sure every sponsor is recognized in the way you promised. I could go on, but the idea is that every tiny little thing you might think doesn't matter, does. Therefore, the decision to execute an event is big one.

Grant Writing

Most nonprofits also utilize grant writing as a way to fundraise and support their work. Grants are simply formal donations that come from corporations, government entities, or foundations. They usually require an application and the attainment of specific goals that the funding will be used to meet. Most grants also require some sort of follow-up reporting once the grant money has been used. Most grants are offered for specific programs or projects, but there are a few that offer general operating support to run your organization.

Grant writing could be an entire book in and of itself (in fact, there are books out there about it). Grant writing is really an art that must be mastered if you are going to obtain grant funding, and is beyond the scope of this book. But I do want to point out some of the most important points to consider when you're thinking about finding and obtaining grant money.

The best way to find available grants is to search for them, usually using the internet. There are a plethora of businesses, governmental agencies, and private and community foundations that offer grants. In fact, many cities or suburban areas have their own community foundations that provide support to local nonprofits. Examples include The Community Foundation for Northern Virginia and the California Community Foundation, which serves Los Angeles County. One of the best resources for finding foundations and subsequent available grants is through the Foundation Center (foundationcenter.org). This site provides a lot of resources and how-to guides as well as an online searchable database for foundations and grants. There is a fee to become a member; but local libraries have subscriptions that anyone can use any time. It's worth a trip to the library to see what's out there.

Read all application information, instructions, and resources available for a grant application, and follow all directions exactly. This may seem a little bit hardcore, but grantors have particular guidelines they want followed. Not following their directions gives them an easy excuse to eliminate your application, so be careful, be thorough, and follow all directions exactly.

Although grant writing is a type of technical writing and requires clear, concise answers to questions, being awarded a grant cannot be whittled down to whether you have the best answers to the provided questions. Funders read and compare grants using specific assessment criteria, but the decision of who to fund often comes down to several qualitative factors like which person read your application, when they read the application (and whether they were tired, hungry, or worried about something personal), whether your application was at the beginning of the pile or the end, and whether or not you know someone in the granting organization.

Don't get discouraged if you don't receive grant funding right away. The key is to keep trying and always follow up with the grantor to see if there was something you could have done or communicated differently. That said, while it's always worthwhile to make revisions to your applications as you learn more about what funders want, know that sometimes it's not about you or your program or your application. Sometimes there simply is not enough funding to go around. Don't take it personally, and don't let it discourage you.

Despite the obstacles, you always want to put your best foot forward when completing a grant application. This is the time to use formal language—avoid contractions, write in third person, and use proper pronouns and correct subject-verb agreement. Make sure the grant is formatted exactly the way the funder wants it. For example, some funders prefer paper applications, stapled or not stapled, printed on one side or two, in a certain font. Others allow you to submit grants online. And some require specific forms you need to complete online in order to apply. Pay close attention, have a good writer proofread your application, and don't make sloppy mistakes.

As for the application itself, answer the questions or

complete the requested information concisely and accurately. Be sure to reread questions as you develop answers to them to make sure you are indeed answering the right query. Don't use flowery or showy language. Simply be direct and succinct, answering what is asked for without expounding where unneeded.

In addition, be on time. Potential grants are often announced months in advance. That not only provides you the time to complete a well-written application but it also ensures you have plenty of time to turn it in. This may seem like a small detail, but funders tend to reject late applications. If your application is due by 5 p.m., it must be turned in by 5 p.m. Otherwise, it might simply be thrown out and not even reviewed. You'd hate for that to happen after a lot of time and effort.

Never hesitate to contact a funder or potential grantor. Always ask questions if you are confused about something on the application. In addition, many private foundations are happy to discuss your ideas before you even apply. They don't want to spend their time reading applications that don't have anything to do with what they want to fund, and you don't want to spend time writing applications for something you have no chance of receiving. Again, if you don't receive a grant, follow up with the funder about why. They may not be able to tell you why, but it's always worthwhile to make a personal connection and show interest in the process. The next time you submit an application, they may remember your tenacity.

Speaking of next time, should you be rejected for funding, always consider submitting another application when the same funder offers grant money again. Do not give up on one funder after one application. The more times they see your organization's name cross their desks, the better your chances for success.

With persistence in mind, also be selective in which grants you apply for. It might seem like a good idea to apply for anything and everything that's available, but that's not the case. First, completing grant applications takes a lot of time and effort. Second, the projects that you are applying for take time and effort too. If there is a grant that allows you to do exactly what you're already doing, great. That means you won't be using extra resources and time for a new project. That happens very rarely. In most cases, you are applying for funding for a new project or program that is going to require additional manpower and resources. While getting the grant can provide that for you, you must assess whether or not your organization has the capacity to take on that new program. In addition, does that new program really go with your mission and goals?

Recently, I was approached to write a very large government grant application for a nonprofit. I immediately read the Request for Proposal (RFP, or the document many funders use to solicit proposals and provide instructions) and saw how complicated and time-consuming it was going to be. The potential funding opportunity was substantial, but it was going to require the creation of an entirely new program. In addition, the application was ridiculously complicated even to access. It was all completed online, and we didn't match many of the possible answer categories, so there was going to be a lot of explaining for us to do. All in all, it was not a good fit. And yet the organization did not agree with me and wanted to apply anyway. Within two weeks, the other person working on the application had abandoned the entire idea because it was too complicated and would require too much time. Go figure.

Some grantors will ask for more than just a written essay type application. Some will ask you to complete graphic models of what your goals are, what you plan to put into them, and what you plan to accomplish. Although many grantors are moving away from these logic models, as they're called, because they don't account for the human element of human services, some still use them. Do not be afraid of these models. Logic models are simply graphic representations of how you've defined these terms for your organization and what the end is going to look like. They are pictures of the goals, objectives, and outcomes you've defined with a smaller number of words. If for no other reason than becoming familiar with them because of potential funding, you and the members of your organization should learn these terms and think through what they mean for your mission. [**On the next page**] is a sample of a basic logic model. This was developed by the W. K. Kellogg Foundation and can be found in their Logic Model Development Guide for free.[8]

Grants are truly about who you know. Although we would all like to think that each funder reviews each grant application without any bias or favoritism, the truth of the matter is that funding is often offered to organizations that have a personal connection to the funder. This can be discouraging in a way, but it can also serve as motivation and a reminder that building relationships is important. The more people you

Basic Logic Model Development Template

Resources	Activities	Outputs	Short- & Long-Term Outcomes	Impact
In order to accomplish our set of activities we will need the following:	*In order to address our problem or asset we will conduct the following activities:*	*We expect that once completed or under way these activities will produce the following evidence of service delivery:*	*We expect that if completed or ongoing these activities will lead to the following changes in 1–3 then 4–6 years:*	*We expect that if completed these activities will lead to the following changes in 7–10 years:*

Outcomes and Impacts should be SMART:

- Specific
- Measurable
- Action-oriented
- Realistic
- Timed

get to know in your community, the better chance you have of finding funding and becoming successful. It's possible the funders will put out a call for applications for brand new organizations and programs, but when they don't, they like to see applications from organizations they are familiar with. They want to be able to go ask someone in another department if and what they've heard about XYZ organization. They like to see organizations with track records of completing programs and achieving goals. This is difficult for new organizations to demonstrate, but persistence and good connections pay off. Ideally, you want someone in the organization encouraging the grant review committee to give money to you.

111

Motivations and Takeaways

- There are a ton of ways to fund your organization, and finding the most successful for you will probably require a lot of trial and error, but building strong relationships outside the organization is the one key to all fundraising strategies.

- Creativity also goes a long way in fundraising, particularly in obtaining individual donations.

- Be discerning about special events and grants. They are definitely worthwhile in many situations, but carefully weigh the amount of the time and effort you have to put into them against the benefit you will be receiving.

- As soon as your organization grows enough to begin hiring employees, you will want to hire someone to focus on fundraising or development as it's called. Having someone dedicated to this area of your organization is key to its success.

CHAPTER 9

Who's Coming with Me?

Employees and Volunteers

Alone we can do so little,
together we can do so much.
—HELEN KELLER

D id you ever see that scene from *Jerry Maguire* in which Jerry (Tom Cruise) decides to leave the company? He's fed up with the company he's working for and decides to go out on his own. Everyone thinks the idea of him leaving is crazy, as he's ranting and raving all over the office and yelling, "Who's coming with me?" No one volunteers to go with him except one sweet, naive colleague who also happens to be in love with him.

Now, I don't think for a minute that your idea is crazy. Quite the contrary. However, I do know that some people might think you've gone and lost it, especially those who wouldn't take a chance on sticking their own necks out for such a cause. A word of caution: those are not your people! You are going to need some other amazing, knowledgeable, reliable souls to be your employees, volunteers, and supporters in this endeavor, so do not rely on those naysayers. In addition, take caution in simply hiring friends or family because they're willing—you need to make sure they have the right skills to run your organization. Remember, head and heart!

Non-Negotiable Paid Positions

As you're starting out, finding and being able to pay the right people will be a challenge. So will prioritizing who to hire and pay first. Let's start there.

You might be a lone workhorse at first, taking care of a range of jobs from paying the bills to overseeing the programs to cleaning the office (if you can finance your organization well, that shouldn't be the case for long). Also, knowing the value of your own time is just as important as recognizing when you don't have the proper skills to execute certain tasks. Therefore, there are two positions that are non-negotiable when it comes to a financial investment in people.

We've spoken already about the necessity and value of legal services. There are simply so many legal requirements and potential areas for mistakes that it makes no sense not to pay for the services of a good lawyer. This will most likely require a monthly retainer fee so that your lawyer is present for you when you need him/her. In addition, you will incur hourly charges when you use his/her services. These can add up, but they're worth it. In addition, many firms will offer discounted rates to nonprofits. Never, ever be afraid to explain your mission and ask for a discount. Keep in mind, though, that pro bono (for free) services are hard to come by and may be of lesser quality because they're being offered for free. This is not always the case, but it's a possibility. Before you assume that you should be able to get something like legal services for free, weigh the quality of the service against the value of your investment in the long run. In addition, you can be judicious with fees if you are organized with your thoughts and tasks when you utilize your lawyer's services.

Again, hire a lawyer. Seriously.

The second position that is a must-pay is an accountant. Most people can do the majority of their bookkeeping and basic accounting themselves. Software has come a long way, and there are loads of easy-to-use programs and applications that can help you run the financials of your business efficiently. Doing the day-to-day banking, check writing, and reconciling of accounts can all be done by you or another nonprofessional volunteer or staff member.

The fact remains that there are many more complex accounting tasks that will be done most efficiently and accurately by a professional accountant. Some of these include assistance in writing a well-planned budget, organizing payroll and taxes, and preparing detailed financial statements. A paid accountant should be able to look at the records objectively and provide the proper expertise to keep the nonprofit organized, honest, and well-prepared for whatever the financial situation may be. In addition, having a paid person in this position rather than a volunteer helps to ensure a sense of responsibility and dependability for an extremely important area of your business.

Of course I want you to be able to count and account for the basics of your business. But unless you are an accountant by profession, many of these details are best left up to some-onewho has professional expertise, particularly when it comes to accounting for nonprofits. An accountant can complete the necessary work accurately and can save you a lot of time, effort, and headaches spent trying to figure out something for which you weren't trained. Always know your numbers and your financial position, but also be willing to allow a professional to take care of the details.

Independent Contractors Versus Paid Employees

Whereas you generally hire a lawyer on retainer, an accountant could be hired as an independent contractor or an employee (more on that later). You may also find it a good idea to hire others as independent contractors, especially when you're starting out and you need someone in a specific position or suited to a particular set of tasks (i.e., accounting, website design, graphic design, a one-time marketing campaign, etc.). Independent contractors are often also referred to as consultants or freelancers. The biggest differences between an independent contractor and an employee of your organization are in compensation and reporting.

Independent contractors sign a contract that allows them to work a certain number of hours in a pay period and are paid either an hourly or flat rate. Organizations hiring independent contractors do not need to withhold federal and state payroll taxes for those people, but must file Form 1099 for each (something an accountant will handle). In addition, independent contractors often work remotely, provide their own

Independent Contractors Versus Employees

LALO Independent Contractors:

Accounting	10 hrs./week @ $30/hr.	$300/wk.
Graphic Design	10 hrs./week @ $30/hr.	$300/wk.
Website/Social Media Manage	15 hrs./week @ $30/hr.	$450/wk.
Marketing/Public Relations	10 hrs./week @ $30/hr.	$300/wk.
Fundraising/Grant Writing	20 hrs./week @ $30/hr.	$600/wk.
Management of contractors	20 hrs./week @ $30/hr.	$600/wk.
Total (85 hrs./week @ $30/hr):		**$2,550/wk.**
Annual Total:		**$132,600/yr.**

Or:

Potential Part-time Employees:

Accounting	10 hrs./week @ $30/hr.	$300/wk.
Position 1	25 hrs./week @ $30/hr.	$750/wk.
Part-time Graphic Design/Website/Social Media Manager		
Position 2	30 hrs./week @ $30/hr.	$900/wk.
Part-time Fundraiser/Grant Writer		
Management of positions	16 hrs./week @ $30/hr.	$700/wk.
Total (81 hrs/week @ $30/hr.):		**$2,430/wk.**
Annual Total:		**$126,360/yr.**
Potential Savings with Part-time Employees:		**$6,240/yr.**

equipment and supplies, and don't work on a set schedule. Organizations do not provide benefits for independent contractors either, so for organizations starting out, independent contractors or freelancers are often the way to go.

Careful here. Independent contractors should sign contracts that are limited to a specific period of time. No benefits should be offered, and extensive training should not be needed for the task at hand. If any of these are not true, the IRS may consider the hire an employee rather than an independent contractor, and different rules will apply. Your lawyer can give you advice on these decisions.

Another caution with respect to independent contractors is that hiring too many of them does not benefit your organization. Although they are a great option for distinct tasks often needed in the short-term, or from someone considered a specialist in a certain area, having a large number of them may actually be a disadvantage to your organization. Financially, independent contractors make a lot of sense, unless you have too many of them, in which case you could actually be wasting money. In addition, each one is a separate team member you have to supervise and communicate with, which gives you a lot to juggle. If you could consolidate several independent contracting jobs into one part-time or full-time employee position, it might make better sense because you'd have fewer people to supervise and coordinate and fewer bills to pay.

Let's look at an example for LALO. Would it make sense to combine any of these independent contractor positions? For argument's sake, let's say we're paying each position the same hourly rate. The truth is, in the real world, you will most likely be negotiating pay rates with each independent contractor.

In this scenario, I could logically combine the web-design and social media duties with the marketing and public relations tasks to form one position. I could do the same with fundraising and grant writing, saving myself or LALO's ED several hours of communication and coordination. This would also allow us to have a more cohesive team that could communicate more easily and, hopefully, even meet together regularly. Financially, this arrangement could potentially save LALO $6,240 per year, as these part-time positions still do not require us to provide benefits.

These decisions depend on a number of factors, including the abilities of the employees you're hiring, your own management experience overseeing employees, the rate at which you're willing to pay employees, and what benefits you're willing to provide. Simply put, it must constantly be a cost-benefit-analysis to see what is best for you and your organization. I simply want to caution you against thinking that having multiple independent contractors can always save money or make sense for your cause. Always do the math!

In the case of hiring paid employees for your organization, there are many rules and regulations. There are federal, state, and local labor laws to follow, and those should be consulted when you are developing your personnel policies, which should always be included in your policies and procedures manual (see Chapter 6). The U.S. Department of Labor (dol.gov) can assist you, as can your lawyer, with determining what you can and cannot require from employees, including particular behaviors, hours worked, and benefits. You will need policies regarding leave, including holidays, vacations, sick time, bereavement, and, possibly, maternity/paternity time. You will need to spell out nondiscrimination policies, whistleblower policies, probationary and evaluation procedures, and termination policies. You will need a well-organized and reliable payroll system and the latest information with which you must abide within the Affordable Health Care Act.[9]

119

The Right Employees

In looking for employees, a word of caution that reminds me of our discussion about board members. While it's wonderful to have friends and family as supporters of your mission and organization, it can easily become messy and awkward if you choose to hire any of them as employees. Many a relationship or friendship has been soured by a poor business deal, in both for- profit and nonprofit businesses alike. It is possible that a friend or family member may have the necessary skills and expertise to fill one of your positions. And it's possible for that partnership to be successful, but only if the responsibilities and expectations of the job are clearly spelled out in writing and agreed to by both of you. Just as you would vet another employee you're considering hiring, you must follow the same procedure with a friend or family member. You should require a resume, relevant experience, and open discussions about what each of you would bring to the table. In addition, a signed contract is the best way to ensure that both of you have at least seen the terms of expectations and responsibilities for the open position. You should provide a copy of that signed contract to the employee along with an orientation packet similar to that which you would give a new board member or volunteer.

With respect to finding reliable, dependable employees with a heart for your cause, there will most likely be some challenges. Starting out, you will not be able to offer competitive salaries or benefits, which will diminish your potential employee pool. Even so, you will have a good opportunity to access those looking for part-time work whom you could use as independent contractors or take on as part-time employees and who may want to work themselves into a full- time position when you grow enough to be able to hire them full-time. In addition, there are some great resources out there for nonprofits looking for individuals looking for jobs, like workforgood.org and idealistcareers.org.

As I mentioned with a friend or family member, make sure that you are vetting all of your potential employees by requiring resumes, references, and relevant experience. Conduct thorough interviews and always check references. Even if you're hiring someone you know, be sure to ask detailed questions about their previous responsibilities, how they met the required workload, and how they demonstrated integrity and professionalism. They may also have some skills of which you weren't even aware, and you always want to use your employees to the best of their abilities.

Allowing them to work to their strengths is not only a benefit to them but also to you. In order to do that, you need to know them and their experiences well. Your organization will be stronger when your employees are working to their potential in the areas they enjoy.

Job Descriptions

Once you decide it's finally time to get some help, the first thing you need to do is create a well-written job description (see sample excerpt below from a recent American Heart Association posting). This should be done before you even advertise what you're looking to fill because the act of creating a job description allows you to brainstorm the skills your new hire must have and the duties for which the position will be responsible. A good description is usually about a page long, depending on what the job entails, and usually includes things like a paragraph describing the job, the level of education required, experience and special skills needed, and the responsibilities of the job spelled out one by one.

Sample Job Description

Responsibilities

We are looking to fill an **Administrative Associate** position who will provide administrative and logistical support to the special event fundraising directors and critical fund-raising events in our **Harrisburg, PA** market.

Your Key Responsibilities will include (but not be limited to):
Administrative and data management: (75-80%)

- data entry into event management systems;
- processing invoices and payments;
- preparing correspondence and spreadsheets,
- informational materials and reports;
- support administrative data for Board of Directors' meetings
- supporting fundraising directors and Executive Director in meetings and at events as needed, (meeting minutes, administrative support) - TBD

Event Logistics: (20-25%)

- coordinating event materials (invitations, brochures, event signage);
- preparing attendee list and tracking registrations;
- working with vendors;
- obtaining required permits;
- attending assigned events to help with set-up and tear down;
- acting as contact person at event site on event day;
- working with the event director to ensure all event-related items are completed in a timely manner.

In this role, you will be based in our Harrisburg office and will report to the Office Manager. You may support 2 or more fundraising directors in the market.
(Reasonable accommodations may be made to enable individuals with disabilities to perform the essential functions.)

Qualifications

If you want to join our team and be a " **Relentless force for a world of longer, healthier lives** ", review the preferred skills and experience we are looking for below: (Reasonable accommodations may be made to enable individuals with disabilities to perform the essential functions.)

- a college degree or some college preferred, at least a high school diploma or GED is required;
- advanced skills in Word, Outlook, Excel and PowerPoint are required;

- strong database management experience;
- experience in administrative support that includes simultaneously supporting multiple directors and/or fundraising events is highly desirable;
- able to work in a fast-paced, time-sensitive environment;
- able to multi-task and organize a heavy workload with minimal supervision;

It's sometimes difficult to determine exactly everything you will want this person to do, especially when you're just starting out. Many job descriptions also contain that little line that says, "Other duties as assigned." While this is a good CYA (Cover Your Ass) line, I caution you to be as detailed as possible in your job description so that both you and your employee know what is expected. However, just because the description is detailed does not mean it is set in stone. If you find, once you've hired someone, that some things are working and some are not, you, the employee, and the board can work together to make changes.

Changes will also likely occur when new employees are brought on in the future. Therefore, these documents are meant to be guides that give your organization structure and divide the workload. Job descriptions also serve an important role in helping you evaluate employee performance, which should be done at regular intervals. Without a written job description, it is difficult to measure employees' progress, achievements, and contributions to the organization. That being said, many organizations are looking to allow employees more self-direction and freedom in what they work on and how they choose to do it. While this idea has merit, it must be considered that the most successful organizations, both for-profit and nonprofit, operate with written job descriptions at every level.

Employees should be included in determining their own

goals and objectives for their positions whenever possible, as that will allow them to have more of an investment in their work as well as higher work satisfaction and work performance. A friend of mine worked for a nonprofit whose goal was to completely do away with job descriptions and allow its employees to determine their goals for themselves. This organization wanted to provide more autonomy for its employees and remove the idea of a top-down management style. While this is an admirable idea that can be enacted in other ways, eliminating job descriptions does not accomplish this and actually benefits no one. Employees began leaving because no one's responsibilities were properly laid out. Multiple people were doing the same jobs while some jobs weren't being covered, and communication wasn't clear.

Job descriptions provide direction and guidelines but also provide efficiency and promote good communication. Without job descriptions, roles become less defined and boundaries become murky. As you grow, employees will not know which tasks are their responsibility versus others, and it will become more complicated and require more steps to keep everyone updated on the status of projects and deadlines.

When you start interviewing, refer to the job description you've written so you can determine whether each candidate has the necessary abilities to fill the position. A job description is key to making sure that both you and your employee know what the expectations and responsibilities are, and it is always best to share these up front as soon as possible. It is imperative that these things are clearly spelled out so that everyone is on the same page. Though job descriptions may not solve all of your problems, having employees sign a contract upon employment stating that they have received and read the job description will serve as some protection against poor job performance, future discrepancies, and arguments about responsibilities.

Flexibility, Food, Fun

Once you hire your employee or employees, it's likely that you won't be able to pay them as much as they are worth—you're a nonprofit startup! But that doesn't mean your team can't be compensated in other ways. The nonprofit industry has long been known for providing other types of benefits, one of the biggest being flexibility. Because of the varied nature and duties of nonprofit work, from serving clients after normal business hours to sweeping floors or cleaning the office, nonprofits often allow employees to set their own schedules, within reason. If there are particular times at which programs are operating and employees must be present, it goes without saying that those hours are required. However, there is no harm in allowing employees to work around those hours with some leeway, whether that means adjusting hours around childcare, appointments, or simply hours of the day in which people work their best (early morning, late afternoon, or evening). When I worked at the Literacy Council of Northern Virginia, I taught English as a Second Language classes to adults from 10–12 p.m. and again from 6–8 p.m. on Tuesdays and Thursdays. Those days felt really long. In order to compensate for what was more than a 9–5 schedule on some days, my other days were much shorter. I would come to the office late or leave early or even take Fridays off if I had worked all of my hours for the week. This was an easy adjustment for me, my colleagues, and my Executive Director because even though my hours were different, they were predictable, and everyone knew when I could be counted on to accomplish my job. This flexibility is one of the easiest and most accommodating things nonprofits can offer their employees, especially when their financial compensation may be less than desired.

Another simple yet valuable asset nonprofits can use to help compensate their employees is food. Yes, this seems too silly to be true, and I'm not talking about providing full meals. Food is a universal language, and it can be used to soothe a lot of what ails nonprofit employees. The occasional party, potluck, or ice cream break can sometimes be the little lift that gets underpaid workers through the day with a smile on their faces. Maybe it's coffee your employees like or a pizza lunch on Fridays. It's a small investment (which you won't even always be responsible for—sometimes your employees will be more than happy to chip in, or a board member might be willing to treat the staff to lunch once in a while) in your employees to make them feel appreciated and thought of.

At LCNV, we did everything from a full-on, potluck Thanksgiving dinner to simple runs to Baskin Robbins for ice cream some afternoons. We celebrated employee birthdays with ice cream cakes, and many times we ordered lunch in for everyone. Another thing that boosted morale were the days when we all sat down to lunch together, even if everyone brought their own lunch. Taking that break during the day was sometimes all we needed to go back to our desks and put our noses back to the grindstone.

And then there's always fun. When there's some flexibility, there's also room for fun things every now and again. I remember one spring afternoon when it was particularly gorgeous, and everyone had spring fever. A colleague mentioned she had a ball in her car, so we had an impromptu 20-minute game of parking lot kickball. It was something so simple, but it made everyone feel great. When the organization grew a bit and had a budget for employee appreciation, we closed the office for a day and took a day trip to an amusement park. Mind you, everyone drove personal cars, we found discounted tickets, and we packed our lunches, but it was the principle that counted. There was always fun to be had at that organization, and that accounted for a lot. That went a long way when hours were long, students were needy, and funds were low.

Finally, I am old school in that I am a fan of handwritten notes. I recognize this is beginning to become a lost art, but I think it's an important one. I force (gently) my own children to write thank you notes for every gift and act of kindness they receive, but I also model that myself. I look forward to receiving such things in the mail myself, and I like to think they make a difference to others. The same can be said when it comes to appreciating your employees. Handwritten notes, emails of appreciation and acknowledgement, and even simple sticky notes of affirmation can make a huge difference.

Volunteers

Volunteers are the nonprofit industry's most valuable asset and liability. Without volunteers, many nonprofits wouldn't even exist, as some operate solely by volunteers. Even large nationwide and worldwide nonprofits use volunteers to help spread their missions, provide services, and perform necessary functions. The Corporation for National & Community Service reports that in 2018, Americans volunteered 6.9 billion hours, the economic value of which was approximately $167 billion (the full report can be found at www.serve.gov.[10] That's no small piece of the economic pie.

The great thing about volunteers is that they can perform almost any task with the proper training. Volunteers comprise nonprofit boards, answer phones, stuff envelopes, and provide direct services like tutoring, coaching, and organizing events, among other things.

One might think, "Well, if volunteers can do all of those things, why would I hire anyone?" The long and short answer to that lies in the idea that you pay for what you get. While volunteers are invaluable to organizations and perform a multitude of jobs, their duties must be spelled out as well as paid employees if not better, records must be kept on their service, and it's difficult to get rid of a volunteer who may not perform at an acceptable level. Ultimately, you may just need more than volunteers can give. Or, you might need a mix of paid employees and volunteers to run your organization most efficiently.

The challenge with volunteers is getting the best out of them for the job. Recruiting, training, and managing volunteers can often become a full-time job in and of itself, so some organizations end up hiring a volunteer coordinator/manager/director. An important thing to note is that whether or not there is a volunteer coordinator, someone must be responsible for creating thorough volunteer job descriptions, locating dedicated volunteers, and performing a thorough interview process to make sure the person in question is a good fit for your organization. In fact, there is an argument that job descriptions and interview processes should be even more thorough than those for paid employees because some volunteers share jobs and volunteers require detailed supervision.

Who are these dedicated volunteers? Well, that depends on what jobs you're looking to fulfill and how many hours you need them. However, there are some attributes that are common to people who spend time volunteering, which can also give you an idea of where to find good volunteers. Believe it or not, chances are that most of your volunteers will not be retirees with lots of spare time. Through a survey sponsored by the Corporation for National and Community Service, data gathered in 2016 told us that in the US, volunteers tend to be married females with higher education levels. They tend to fall into the 35–44 year-old age group and most likely have children under 18, and most of these volunteers are working with one or two organizations a year[11]. Those facts can help you determine where to look for your volunteers and where to focus your recruitment efforts.

Since parents with children tend to get more involved than any other demographic, it follows that anywhere you can find children, you can find parents and, therefore, potential volunteers. Targeting women's and parents' organizations would be great places to start. Keep in mind, though, that while statistically these are the most common volunteers, you'll want to look at other sets of people as well, including men and other age groups. People volunteer for many reasons, including helping the community, helping their friends, making new friends, and trying new things. People also like to polish their resumes with volunteer opportunities as well as develop new skills. One very common place to find people who are interested in volunteering is VolunteerMatch.org. As an organization, you can post your volunteer opportunities, and volunteers can search and find opportunities that fit them. You can use their basic service for free, and they offer a more upgraded service for $10/month.

Once volunteers are taken on, the job of managing them becomes ongoing. Volunteers need orientation to your organization and training on what they need to do and how it needs to be done. Lists of responsibilities and expectations are important as is a volunteer agreement form, similar to an employee contract (see next page for a sample). It's helpful to have a volunteer orientation packet, just as you have a similar one for new board members. Volunteers must be covered by your organization's insurance, and their tasks and hours must be recorded for financial purposes.

Volunteer hours are worth an amount provided by the Independent Sector, a national membership organization for the charitable community, so that organizations who use volunteers can calculate the monetary value of a volunteer's time. In April of 2019, the Independent Sector released the new value for volunteers as $25.43/hour.[12] Logging the hours your volunteers provide for your organization allows you to correctly calculate the worth of the work you're receiving for free. This value is not just for your records but also can be used to show others how well you are leveraging your assets.

Volunteer Agreement

SLS SAMPLE DOCUMENT 06/27/17

Thank you for helping us to [_____]. Client would not be able to [_____] without the dedication and passion of volunteers like you.

In line with and in consideration with your participation as a volunteer, we ask you to confirm your understanding and agreement to the following:

- You agree, for your own safety and that of others, that you will comply with Client's volunteer policies, safety rules, and other directions, and will supervise any child or other person for whom you are responsible.

- You assume full responsibility for any and all risks that may arise from your presence at Client program sites or participation in Client activities. These include risks arising from physical exertion, lifting heavy objects, conditions at facilities, using sharp objects or other tools, traveling to or from a program site, or interacting with students, other volunteers, or others.

- You agree to waive and release any claims against Client and its directors and employees, including any claims for death or for injury to your person or property, resulting from your participation as a Client volunteer.

- You authorize Client to provide you first aid, emergency medical assistance, and transportation.

- You agree to hold in confidence at all times, during and after participation, any confidential information you have access to as a volunteer of Client, and to use and disclose such information only as expressly authorized by Client.

- You grant full and exclusive rights to Client in any works you may create in the course of volunteer activities, and in any brochures, posters, reports, websites, software, presentations, or other materials you create or help to create for Client, including any intellectual property rights in or derivatives of such materials.

- You consent to use of your image, voice, name, or story by Client, for purposes of promotion and fundraising, on its website, in its publications, through social media, or any other media. You agree that you have no right to approve or receive payment for such use, and to waive any legal claims related to such use, including claims relating to copyright or rights of publicity or privacy. If you do not wish to agree to this consent, please check this box: ☐

- You understand that you are not an employee of Client and will not be paid for participation as a volunteer or be eligible for participation in Client's benefit plans.

- You understand this agreement applies throughout the duration of your participation as an Client volunteer, and that this agreement is complete and supersedes all prior or contemporaneous communications or understandings between you and Client relating to volunteer activities.

- You have read this agreement and understand its terms. You sign it freely and voluntarily.

Thank you again for volunteering with Client.

Volunteer Name	Volunteer Signature	Date
Parent's/Guardian's Name (if under 18)	Parent's/Guardian's Signature	Date
Emergency Contact Name	Relation to Volunteer	Phone

It can be used to show the community how much you can get accomplished with your limited resources, and it can be used in funding applications to show other organizations how much value you can leverage.

An important thing to note is that good record keeping

will be key. Chances are, you will want your volunteers to sign in and sign out, whether on paper or electronically, so you can track their hours. You may also want to capture their activities, so you know where that time is going. A good practice is to total up those hours at the end of every month so that you don't have to do 12 months' worth at the end of the year.

Volunteers must be managed and supervised skillfully. The dance between volunteers and employees is a delicate balance of service, power, and appreciation. Many times volunteers outlast staff members, serving as institutional memory. As volunteers experience this turnover, they realize they are the constants. They may be the only ones who can explain the nuances of the programs they're serving or the ins and outs of ways things need to be done. This can lead to an imbalance of power between employees and volunteers, particularly when employees have been put in charge of managing volunteers. These relationships can be difficult to manage, as volunteers need to feel appreciated and valued while certain program requirements and standards need be upheld.

When I came to work at the Literacy Council of Northern Virginia (LCNV), I was tasked with teaching several ESL classes as well as overseeing the volunteers also teaching at those class locations. Many volunteers were used to being supervised by rotating employees and understood where their duties began and ended. Most were happy simply teaching a class and turning in the necessary paperwork to me on time. However, there were two volunteers—a husband and wife couple who we'll call Mr. and Mrs. Smith—who had been volunteering for years. They practically ran the site location where they taught, and they made it clear to whoever the incoming staff member was that they were in charge. They had developed some bad habits, though, and things had slowly started to go off the rails. Policies weren't being followed, which led to unfairness in registering new students. The assessment tool used to assign students to different levels of classes was being used incorrectly, despite repeated trainings on how to administer it. What made things difficult was the fact that Mr. and Mrs. Smith were the most dedicated, generous, and giving set of volunteers the organization had. Not only that, but they were also huge givers financially. So, handling them delicately was a trip, for sure.

It took time and consistency, but I eventually won those volunteers over. It took repeated trainings, reinforcement of policies, and explanations why things were done the way they were. It also took a lot of compliments, demonstrations of appreciation, and proving of myself to make things run smoothly again. After all, I was a very young 20-something, fresh out of college, coming to tell adults several decades my senior how to run their volunteer jobs. I had to be very careful when to say something and when to let something slide, when to enforce something and when to let it go, and when to change things and when to leave them alone. Consistency was key, as was calm in the face of frustration even when I wanted to smack someone or something. The following year, I became the manager of the classroom program, so I was very much their boss. Because I had proven myself over the previous year and always been polite, willing to listen, and encouraging, they finally took me seriously and took the time to understand why I wanted to make the changes to the program that I did, and that those changes didn't have to be catastrophic for them.

Just as in my example, some of the things that go a long way with volunteers include being willing to listen, always being polite, and being complimentary whenever possible. Appreciate either the institutional knowledge or personal experience of volunteers and rely on them for information you may not know. Show them that you care by saying thank you, especially through an annual recognition event of some type. You may give small gifts or tokens of appreciation, and public acknowledgement is always helpful. Never disregard the value of written thank you notes, even at regular intervals throughout the year. At LCNV, we had four class sessions yearly, and we recognized our volunteers at the end of each of them. Sometimes we bought a small token, perhaps a $10 gift card or a nice pen or trinket. One time we decided we were tired of store-bought things and chose to make bags of trail mix for each volunteer. That turned out to be pretty fun because it became a group activity to make the trail mix and assemble the bags, and the volunteers were particularly appreciative of something homemade. Never discount the small things.

I've also been on the other side, volunteering for many nonprofit organizations throughout my career. As a volunteer, I wanted to give my time freely and also wanted direction, guidance, and autonomy at the same time. I definitely wanted to feel appreciated even though I did most of my volunteer work for personal fulfillment. Some of my favorite volunteer jobs have been language interpreting in a free medical clinic and distributing food at a local food bank. I've also had some not-so-good experiences. These were always characterized by chaotic environments with leaders who were disorganized and haphazard, jumping from one 'best' idea to another. In these cases, I have gotten frustrated easily, particularly when assigned a specific task I spent time and effort on only for it to be thrown to the side without a glance later. I can promise you one way to piss off a volunteer quickly is to assign them something then not use it!

Building an organization is tough. Finding the right people to work with, whether paid or unpaid, is a challenge that is not unique to you, but a challenge, nonetheless. The relationships between employers, employees, and volunteers can be tenuous and must be handled effectively. However, when you find the right people, your organization can make tremendous strides in growth and success.

Motivations and Takeaways

- Invest the time and resources to hire good legal and accounting staff. Though they may be significant expenses, they will pay off many times over in the long run.

- Consider the use of independent contractors, especially as you're getting started. Always assess the pros and cons of such plans over hiring employees. Be sure, no matter which way you go, that you are legally and financially sound.

- Be very cautious when considering hiring friends or family, if you hire them at all.

- Be sure to use detailed job descriptions for employees and volunteers so that everyone's roles and responsibilities are explained thoroughly.

- Find creative ways to compensate your employees and volunteers and always make sure they feel appreciated.

- Use volunteers to their fullest potential while making sure they are cared for and appreciated.

CHAPTER 10

Where Are We Going?

Goal Setting
& Strategic Planning

Our goals can only be reached through the vehicle
of a plan, in which we must fervently believe,
and upon which we must vigorously act.
There is no other route to success.

—PABLO PICASSO

I've always been a list person. Ever since I was old enough to record homework assignments, I've written to-do lists and happily crossed items off. I've even been known to add things to my list that weren't originally on it just to get that rush of checking them as "done." That small act of accomplishment helps propel me through my day and gives me the motivation to tackle more stuff. Needless to say, it also helps me remember what I need to do and where I'm going.

Lists also make sense to me for my weekly and monthly tasks and goals, both personal and professional. I like the structure, and I also benefit from seeing my goals in writing and being strategic about meeting them. It means thinking in terms of outcome, where I'm going or where I want to be, and how I'm going to get there.

Although it might seem basic to point out, your organization needs this kind of structure too. It's going to become its own entity, and it requires its own lists of goals, objectives, and a long- range plan for where you and your board want it to be in the future.

Goal Setting: Where?

We're all familiar with the word "goal" and the idea of a goal as what you want to accomplish, something you're aiming for, the end you're trying to reach. What many people get confused about is the difference in the overall goals of a nonprofit versus a for-profit organization. The goal of a for-profit organization is, first and foremost, to make money (profits). Those profits then get turned into increased salaries, bonuses, or stockholder dividends. The goal of a nonprofit is to help the community in some way. Nonprofits also have to make money, and that money is used to further the mission of the organization. In other words, after salaries and other expenses are paid, instead of giving raises or bonuses or dividends, nonprofits put any leftover money back into the organization to build its programs, people, and services.

Beyond the overall goal of a nonprofit to help the community or a for-profit to make money, both types of organizations must set goals to achieve within that framework. In other words, how are they going to fulfill their mission? Generally, goals for your organization look a lot like dreams or aspirations. They cast a big and wide net, encompassing your overall intentions for the organization. They come directly from your mission and should always be aligned with your mission.

For example, the mission of the Literacy Council of Northern Virginia is to teach adults the basic skills of reading, writing, speaking, and understanding English so they can access employment and educational opportunities and more fully and equitably participate in the community. One of its goals is to teach English Language Learners (ELLs) to speak, understand, read, and write English. Another one of its goals is to teach immigrants the foundational language, literacy, and cultural skills needed to obtain, succeed, and advance in entry level jobs. These goals are based on the organization's mission statement and carried out through its different programs. Not only can the organization as a whole have goals, but each program and even each employee should also have goals within the greater institution. Goals tell us where we're aiming for, where we want to end up. On a road trip, we usually set a goal for a destination. We decide where we're going first before we decide how we will get there. Goals give us structure and purpose while allowing us the leeway to decide how we will accomplish them. Without goals, both people and organizations tend to wander aimlessly, even work in circles without accomplishing much of anything. With goals, we have intentions, a focus, and a reason to move forward. Goals are both fundamental and motivating, and writing them down promotes even more success. In fact, a study cited by *Forbes* magazine found that people who very vividly describe or picture their goals are anywhere from 1.2 to 1.4 times more likely to successfully accomplish their goals. The same goes for organizations. If you want to get where you're trying to go, you're much more likely to get there if you write down the specifics and focus on them.[13]

Can you think of what some goals might be for our Lemon Aid for Little Ones example? Do you remember the mission we created? We decided it was to provide the community with opportunities to support the Child Life Program at Penn State Hershey Children's Hospital through donations to and volunteer support of its lemonade stands locally. Based on that, what could a possible goal or two be? The first one that comes to my mind is to raise money each month for the local children's hospital. A second goal might be to find additional ways to support the Child Life program at the local children's hospital. Given these ideas, take a minute to think about your own mission statement and what some potential goals for your organization will be. Two to three goals for the organization as a whole is an appropriate aim. Think big in terms of where you want the organization to go, and don't be afraid to aim high. Consider your overarching theme and what you want the organization's accomplishments to be.

Strategy and Objectives: How?

Once you have several goals set, you must figure out how you're going to achieve them. This is where both strategy and objectives come in. Strategy is the method by which you are going to achieve a goal. For example, many, many people set the goal of losing weight. Their strategies are how they decide to do that. One person may choose a specific plan like

Weight Watchers or Jenny Craig. Another may focus solely on going from a very sedentary lifestyle to a very active one. Still another might decide that she will try the new craze of intermittent fasting. These are all ways to achieve the desired aim of losing weight—they are simply different ways to get there. For LALO, our primary strategy for raising funds for the children's hospital is by selling lemonade. We may end up branching out or finding additional ways to reach our goals, but selling our product (or asking for donations for our product) is our primary way to fulfill what we set out to do.

Once you've decided how you'd like to go about achieving your goal, you're going to need to break it into smaller, more manageable chunks or objectives. Although some places use the words "goals" and "objectives" interchangeably, for our purposes we're going to differentiate objectives as small steps your organization takes in order to achieve its goals. If the goal is the end game, the objectives are the less lofty but equally as important accomplishments on the way there. Referring to the weight loss example, many people set a goal of losing a large number of pounds over the course of several months or even a year. But in order to track progress and keep themselves motivated, people break down that larger aim into smaller targets for shorter time periods, for example, two pounds per week. Not only does this allow people (and organizations) to start seeing progress toward an end, but it also spurs motivation to continue to strive toward something larger.

Objectives should also be measurable or quantifiable in some way. Just like the two pounds per week example for weight loss, an organizational objective may be to serve a certain number of clients per week or month toward an annual goal. Objectives need to be set in each area of business in order for the entire organization to reach a goal. To fund the activities to serve the clients you want to, you will also need to find money. Therefore, an objective to bring in a certain amount of money each month is also a common objective of many organizations. If your organization is growing and you need more manpower, an objective might be to bring on or train a certain number of volunteers per month or other time period.

For LALO, objectives might look like this:

- Hold two lemonade stands per month or raise a certain amount of money per month.
- Find two new volunteers each month to hold lemonade stands.
- Make a donation of at least $50 in cash or kind to the Child Life Program each month.

Outcomes: Why?

The goal is where you're going. The strategy is how you're going to get there. The objectives give you a way to measure and quantify your progress, to see how close you're getting to your goal. But why are you headed here in the first place? What are you doing this for, after all?

This is where outcomes come in. Outcomes are similar to goals because they come at the end and explain the end result or product. If you can think of your goals as your overarching aims, the outcomes are what you achieve by getting there. We use outcomes to measure whether or not we've met or are meeting our goals. Goals can sometimes be less quantifiable and more abstract, such as LCNV's goal of teaching people English. But that leaves out the details like how many people, over how long, and how do we define teaching? Outcomes give us the answers to these questions and provide us with a more thorough evaluation of whether or not we've accomplished what we want. For LCNV, some outcomes could look like this:

- How many students took English class this session?
  - ▷ We taught 60 people English.

- How long was the class session or how many hours of instruction were given?
  - ▷ 10-week class session of two-hour classes twice per week = 40 hours.

- How many students moved up a class level?
  - ▷ Out of 60 students, 20 students tested out of the level of class they were in and moved up to the next level.

- How many students achieved a goal they set for themselves?
  - ▷ Each student set his/her own goals, and 45 of them achieved one or more of those goals.

- Were enough funds raised to support the programs?
  - ▷ Yes, and it will cost $XYZ to run the next class session.

- Were there enough paid or volunteer staff to run the programs?
  - ▷ No. Although we pieced together teachers for one of the classes, we were short one position. For next session, we will need an additional volunteer.

In addition to defining these things for the sake of the organization, so that you're more likely to meet your goals, you will often find these terms referred to in grant applications you must use to apply for funding (refer back to Chapter 8). Most grantors want to know exactly what your goals are, how you're going to achieve them, and how you're going to measure them. It's much easier for grantors to put a price tag on outcomes they can count or analyze numerically rather than ones that are only described in stories.

Strategic Planning: When?

Ok. You've got your mission, your goals, your objectives, and your outcomes. You've most likely thought about the programs you're going to create to achieve those goals because at least one, and maybe only one, of those programs came directly from the idea you had to help or serve others in a particular way. Now, have you thought about a timetable? When do you think these things are going to happen? What is a realistic time in which you'll achieve some of these objectives?

Strategic planning is a process you'll need to go through with your organization many times over the course of its life. Strategic planning is planning for the future with an eye toward what will be changing inside and outside your organization. It requires both internal and external assessments of conditions as well as critical thought about how the organization will move forward, taking into consideration the changing nature of the environment, the organization, and its partners, stakeholders, and competition. Strategic planning is necessary as the organization is starting out so that there is a plan for how to begin accomplishing your goals. Strategic planning is usually revisited every few years to determine if the organization is still solving a problem that exists, if its programs and activities are still addressing its mission, and if it needs to grow and adapt and, if so, how. Strategic planning is usually organization-wide, encompassing the founder, members of the board, and members of the staff.

One of the most common strategic planning tools is called a SWOT analysis, which stands for Strengths, Weaknesses, Opportunities, and Threats. Most organizations sit together, often with a neutral facilitator and agreed-upon ground rules, and define and discuss these things one at time. There are consulting firms that can provide facilitators for these types of things, but there are also people who will volunteer. Others who work in nonprofits might be willing to give a few hours to this process for you if you do the same for them. Many retired nonprofit executives are also willing to provide their time and expertise. This is one of those times when networking with others in your field will be key.

As for the analysis itself, strengths are fairly straightforward—these would be the assets your organization has. Do you have qualified staff? Do you provide a necessary and quality service? Do you have different areas of expertise covered on your board? Is your board active and helpful? You'll want to look at each aspect of the organization and try to determine what benefits each has. It's important to be honest through this entire process, even when it's tempting to put the best face of the organization on when undergoing an analysis like this. Don't inflate any strengths the organization has because overstating these things will only serve to hurt you in the long run.

Weaknesses are the opposite of strengths. They're what your organization lacks or can do better. It is important to note that both strengths and weaknesses are internal analyses of the organization. You'll be looking directly inside at what the organization and its people have to offer, not at any external circumstances. For example, a weakness might be that your cost for providing a service is higher than a similar organization's. This is not the same as the overall program costs increasing several percent over the last several years. You have little control over outside costs to the organization to run a program, and that may very well affect your cost to provide the service, but you can only control the cost you charge clients, not the effects that the outside environment has on your costs. Therefore, your higher cost is a weakness, but the increasing costs for you to provide the services are a threat.

Threats are things that are going on externally that have a negative effect on the organization. For example, if you were running a manufacturing business and the goods you make require a certain raw material such as corn, a threat to your organization could be rising costs of buying corn. This is something you have no control over—you have no influence over the corn market, but you need that corn to produce your product.

The same goes for nonprofits. In considering threats, you must think of the things over which you have no control and decide how they affect your organization. A threat has a negative effect on your organization, whereas an opportunity is something going on outside the organization that has a positive effect on the organization. Examples of opportunities could include a scenario in which another agency that serves the same client base you do is closing, which would leave you with additional clients to serve. Another example of an opportunity would be if another organization or the government decided to offer grants for which you could apply. You may or may not receive the grant depending on your application, but the fact that it is available to you could be a favorable circumstance with a positive effect on your organization.

A thorough SWOT analysis can inform your organization of all of the possibilities as well as potential challenges it might face. It can provide a good look at the areas in which you are doing well, the ones in which you need to grow, and positive environmental happenings that might be good for you, as well as things you need to look out for. Note that in a SWOT analysis, one thing may fit into a couple of categories. Something you see as a strength of the organization may also be a weakness in another light. It's important to acknowledge both.

Once you've completed a SWOT analysis, it becomes much easier to determine a plan for the organization. You can break down each category and take items one by one, determining how you will deal with them and what your strategies are going to be to accomplish your goals. You'll want to start putting your plan in writing so it's available to everyone in the organization. And remember that part about writing down your goals to make them more likely to be accomplished? Your goals are going to be included in your plan, and for every time and place you write them down, see them, and share them, the more likely it is that you are going to be successful.

The Strategic Plan

Remember how we talked about the benefits of putting your goals in writing? Once you've determined where you're going, how you're getting there, and what challenges might stand in your way, it's imperative that you write these things down as well. Putting your plan in writing is not only a good exercise for the organization as a whole, but it also strengthens the possibility of accomplishing what you want. It also provides a document you can share and refer to with new staff, board members, potential donors, and various stakeholders. I'm a big fan of three-ring binders for important organizational documents, so my recommendation is to write out your plan formally and keep it accessible to the entire organization in a central location inside a binder with a label. That way everyone has the opportunity to refer to it whenever necessary. Of course always have several back up electronic copies as well, but one hard copy is great for everyone.

So what should it say? These are some things that common strategic plans have.

- Executive summary
- Mission statement
- Description of the planning process used
- Organizational Goals for specific time periods (e.g., five years)
- Results of SWOT analysis
- Based on SWOT analysis, strategies to achieve stated goals
- Appendices that include any background material

used to determine the plan, including a list of people who helped in creating it

This list of things to include might look a little intimidating. But broken down and taken one step at a time, it can be done without much blood, sweat, or tears. One of the most important things to remember is to avoid jargon, catch phrases, big flowery language, and the itch to use complicated, impressive words. You want to make sure you communicate your goals and activities clearly and concisely. It's important to be precise so that when a reader finishes reading your plan, he or she knows exactly what you do, how you do it, why you do it, and why you are the best choice to do it.

Don't forget, these plans should be revisited at least every other year, if not annually. That doesn't mean they have to be amended each year, but they should be reviewed to make sure you are still on track with your goals. The National Council of Nonprofits has some great strategic planning resources.

This chapter is very much focused on the necessary things that require a lot of thinking and brain power. Don't let that deter you from the mission in your heart. You can marry the two in many ways, as we'll see in upcoming chapters.

Motivations and Takeaways

- Come up with two to three specific organizational goals, and write them down in as many places as you can.

- Break each goal down into several smaller, measurable objectives.

- Develop the outcomes that will define whether

or not you've met your goals. Be specific, measurable, and relevant.

- Bring your staff and board together to write a strategic plan for the next several years, including a thorough SWOT analysis. Write your strategic plan as clearly and concisely as possible.
- Revisit your plan at least every other year, if not annually, to determine whether you're still on track to meet your goals.

CHAPTER 11

What Did You Say?

Communication Inside
and Outside

*The single biggest problem in communication is
the illusion that it has taken place.*
—GEORGE BERNARD SHAW

One of the principal ideas of this book has been and
continues to be the idea that there are many business principles from the for-profit sector that should
be applied to the nonprofit sector, but often aren't; that nonprofits use their hearts, but not their heads. There are many
guesses as to why this is true—the nonprofit industry doesn't
see itself as being as worthy, as legitimate as the for-profit; the
nonprofit sector is more "casual" than the for-profit; and the
nonprofit industry doesn't have the money to spend on things
that for-profits do. Some nonprofits don't want to be viewed
as people view for-profits. These issues, among others, only
serve to create more division between the two sectors. There

are actually many similarities between them, and they would both benefit from more collaboration.

In this chapter, we're going to focus on communication, something the for-profit business sector tends to do better than the nonprofit industry. But there's no reason it has to be that way. If you can put any of these ideas into practice, your clear communication can greatly benefit your organization on the inside as well as garner the organization more respect and consideration from the outside.

There are many important aspects to communication, and we're going to cover a few. One of the most important and influential is consistency. As Albert Einstein said, "I speak to everyone in the same way, whether he is the garbage man or the president of the university." To me, this means that no matter who you're communicating with, whether it be someone within or outside of your organization, they must be treated the same way. This is also a good general principle to conduct business by, one my grandfather instilled in me. As a busy CEO of an international company, he had plenty of meetings with distinguished, renowned people. However, he treated them with the same level of respect with which he treated the staff who swept the factory floor or took out the garbage. With respect to communication, the type of communication you would have with your best stakeholder, biggest donor, or most important client is the type of communication that everyone deserves from your organization. That is not to say that you must be on guard in every internal email or send eloquent, well-crafted memos all of the time. It is to say that each person deserves the same amount of respect, and this will be demonstrated throughout many aspects of your organization, but communication is always where it will be the most visible and obvious.

What do I mean by consistency? I mean keeping the following in mind and using them in every communication, every time, whether electronic, written, or verbal:

- Being prompt
- Being clear and concise throughout
- Using the same tone with each person
- Paying close attention to grammar and spelling
- Taking time to proofread and edit where necessary
- Using business language where possible
- Being discerning about when to call and when to write

Let's break these down a bit and determine how they would look for you.

Be prompt. This means returning calls in 1–2 days and returning emails in 2–3 days. If you're out and can't respond, you should leave an out-of-office message or automatic reply with directions to contact someone else in an emergency. If you find you can't respond in a timely manner, sending a quick email saying that you've received the communication and will get back to the sender when you can makes a very good impression and buys you some time. Make sure you do get back to people when you've promised. It is so very important for the integrity and trust inside and outside your organization that you do not break your promises, and don't promise things you can't do.

Be clear and concise. This means you should always get to your point as quickly as possible without trying to be crafty or wordy. Simply convey a clear message using active verbs and uncomplicated words. You should explain or request one thing at a time, noting specific action steps. You do not need to send separate emails for every single request. However, beware of making emails too long, as readers lose interest and forget too many requests. In the online writing world, people frequently use the acronym TLDR to denote, "Too Long, Didn't Read." That applies to offline communication too. Another thing that helps me to remember this is focusing on the phrase, "Say what you mean and mean what you say." If I can prompt myself to think of this phrase, I can more easily stick to my point.

Use a pleasant, polite tone. It is imperative for communication both inside and outside the organization that you always address others kindly and courteously. The old saying that you catch more flies with honey than vinegar is true, and in this case, we're catching your goals and the people and requests you want to attract and attain. Kindness will always get you further than a sour attitude, even when you feel frustrated or upset. Stay aware that often, electronic communication makes it more difficult for readers to determine your tone. So it truly does benefit you and your organization to be careful of wording, eliminate sarcasm, and simply be kind. Your tone can always range from formal to more informal depending on the situation, but your volunteers and employees should follow your lead. All members of your organization should use similar language when writing or speaking about your organization and what it does. You should always be echoing and supporting each other's sentiments, particularly to those outside the organization.

Pay close attention to grammar and spelling. This is something that I cannot stress enough. This should go without saying, but this is one area in which people get lazy, especially in the nonprofit world, where organizations and employees aren't held to the same standards as for-profit businesses. In the for-profit sector, there is constant competition to be able to provide a product or service. If a company wants to make money, it must be the best, or at least better than its competitor. It must show its best in every way, including communication. In profit-making companies, mistakes in grammar and spelling often aren't tolerated. They are pointed out and critiqued and corrected, with continued mistakes resulting in changes of duties or demotions because those mistakes could mean loss of profit. Nonprofits don't have that luxury for several reasons. Primarily, there are fewer competitors because nonprofits are filling gaps in service and people need them. Secondarily, nonprofits don't usually have a pool of people waiting for open jobs. They often can't afford to fire employees over grammatical errors. In addition, it's often difficult for nonprofit staff members who not only have to serve as managers and program personnel but also human resources and service providers, among other things, to cover all of the details every time. When time and resources are spread thin, some things, like grammar and spelling, can fall through the cracks.

I'm here to implore you not to let that happen. I recently just cringed over an email from a nonprofit that was marketing its annual fundraising event. I was completely off-put because the speaker's title—a fairly big, important, and well-known educator—was inconsistent in its capitalization: one time it was capitalized, and one time it wasn't. I know this is a small mistake that would most likely not deter throngs of people from attending the event, but it left a poor taste in my mouth. It made me feel like the announcement was done hastily, or that the writer didn't take the speaker's title seriously, and perhaps the event might be put together hastily as well. It made me question the organization's attention to detail.

So, grammar and spelling are too important to be overlooked. Proper grammar and spelling convey a message that the subject is important, the receiver is worthwhile, and that the writer pays attention to detail. It shows that thought and effort was put into the form of communication, and that implies that the same thought and effort will be put into a reply and continued communication. Errors in grammar and spelling telegraph sloppiness, lack of attention to detail, and carelessness. Just because you are low on manpower does not mean you can slack in areas such as these. There are so many resources available to check grammar and spelling that mistakes truly should not be tolerated.

Proofreading and editing are non-negotiable. I could just write, "See above" here, but this is too important not to highlight. Due to how quickly the world moves today, how fast information is fired at us and we fire it back to others, and how quickly our language and technology changes, it is so very easy to make mistakes, both in grammar and spelling and in wording, comments, and intended recipients. It's critical to proofread your written communications. This applies to any written communication—emails, social media postings, letters, memos, and even Tweets, Snaps, and Instagram posts. It takes a brief time to reread things you write and edit them as necessary, but it saves a lot of pain and misunderstanding in the long run. Simple mistakes can cost organizations money, relationships, time, and manpower. If you have the luxury of multiple people working in your organization or office, it's a best practice—and easy—to have a second person review whatever it is you have written. That person can help look for mistakes, make sure you're communicating the message you're intending to, and make sure your tone is consistent. Do not underestimate the power of proofreading!

Use business language where possible. Something you may have to get used to or learn a bit about is knowing what business language to use and when to use it. That might sound intimidating, and it might feel awkward at first, but it doesn't have to be difficult. This doesn't mean you need a business degree or formal training. It simply means learning to recognize, understand, and become familiar with some common business- and industry-specific terms that apply to your organization. It is less about changing the structure of how you speak and write and more about learning the appropriate vocabulary, both for conducting business and for working in the specific subject area in which you want to run your nonprofit. The Foundation for Enhancing Communities has a very good, simple glossary of common nonprofit terms you should be familiar with.[14] You should also have your accountant and lawyer to rely on when getting into the details of finance and law. The best way to become familiar with appropriate business terms is to read and listen to others, noting words you are unfamiliar with and learning them. Not every business term will apply to you, but the more exposure you have to business terms, the better.

In addition, it might take just a bit of time and research

157

to find out what type of language is commonly used in what will be your organization's area of expertise. For example, if you want to start a program that feeds children after school, you will want to look at similar programs to see what kind of vocabulary and phrasing they are using to describe their programs and their clients. Are they speaking more about food or feeding? What is the current term for children who need food—is it hungry, food insecure, or something else? For LALO, since we want to work with children's hospitals and Child Life programs, we could do some research to find out what similar programs are called in other hospitals, how they refer to children who are patients, and how they refer to families.

When we learn the business terms that other organizations in our subject area use, we refer to them as industry standards, and we can be consistent with each other and other organizations like ours. This helps make things easier when it comes to communicating with other businesses, applying for funding through things like grant applications, and making reports to your clients, board members, and other stakeholders. All of this being said, there is really never any need for flowery, showy language or heavy business jargon. Clear, concise language always wins out over a show of complicated vocabulary.

Another important aspect of communication that has become especially blurry in recent years of electronic communication is deciding when to call versus when to write, or what form of communication to use. This decision needs to be made frequently, sometimes several times a day. Some things are best handled by a phone call, whereas others are best handled quickly and efficiently via email. Sometimes this is easy to determine. Quick questions, things with simple answers, and program questions can often and easily be answered by email. Communication with current clients, board members, and stakeholders can often be dealt with electronically. When it comes to new clients, board members, and stakeholders, it's always best to make a personal call. This applies when someone shows interest in your program, when someone new needs a service, and when someone is interested in providing donations or funding. In these cases, a personal touch can never be overrated. Although our world has moved quickly into an era of near-total online communication, there are still times when connection should be made more personal. This also applies if you're trying to find funding. It's always possible to inquire about things via email, but making a call and speaking to a real person on the other end lays the groundwork for a relationship. When you're hoping to find some money, it's always best to begin building relationships.

An important note of caution when it comes to written communication. It's tempting to turn to social media here, and it can, indeed, be a great tool. It allows us to reach people we never would have been able to reach before, and it can be a huge asset in marketing. Nonetheless, it should never be used for communication with clients, board members, or stakeholders of any kind. While it's fine to make general announcements on social media, it's never OK to communicate information about the organization's inner workings through Facebook, Twitter, Instagram, Snapchat, and whatever new platform arises. Certain things must be kept confidential, and nothing that goes into social media is ever confidential. In addition,

159

some things are simply inappropriate to communicate through social media. These would include financial details, funding prospects, human resource topics, anything about employees, clients, volunteers, or board members, and many other things. It is best to maintain the integrity of the organization by communicating mainly through phone calls and email, no matter how popular social media becomes.

Be careful about electronic communication regarding personnel or human resource matters. If you need to deal with an employee issue, it's always best to speak face-to-face. Employees feel valued and appreciated when they are complimented and encouraged in person. And when problems arise, face-to-face communication keeps matters where they should be: between the manager or director or board of directors and the employee, not among the rest of the staff. If there are matters that an employee has not dealt with properly, a discussion between the manager and employee should take place. Should a policy or procedure be broken, it must be addressed one on one. Once the issue has been dealt with, it's a good idea to follow up via email, putting in writing what was discussed.

Finally, when dealing with personnel issues, a particular communication concern is keeping good records. Because most things are electronic, copies exist in cyberspace and can often be recovered. You must still be judicious about saving copies of any electronic communications. Not only must you be vigilant about keeping records of communications, but you must also be vigilant about recording details of conversations and actions when you have concerns about employees or volunteers not following policies and procedures. Documentation of any questionable behavior is key to providing evidence of the behavior when you have a face-to-face conversation with the employee. In this particular case, I'm referring to general documentation of behavior (how often an employee is late, for example) so that you have evidence to demonstrate a repeated behavior. In addition, I'm referring to documentation of things like job descriptions, policies, and procedures. Those things should always be written down for reference and because they serve as proof of the organization's ways of doing business, rules, and expectations. When you have those things documented and you've shared them with employees and volunteers, they cannot come back to you and tell you they weren't aware of how something is done.

There is another aspect to documentation, and that has to do with your particular industry or specialty. First of all, there will be documentation requirements for your accounting and financials, and your accountant will be the person to explain those to you and tell you what records you need to be sure to keep. Secondly, there will be legal documentation that will need to be maintained, and that can be explained to you by your lawyer. But there may also be certain standards by which your particular subject area requires documentation of services, clients, etc. These requirements may come from state or local agencies, funders, or partner organizations. It is imperative to make yourself aware of any documentation requirements you might face.

For example, if LALO receives a grant to hold a certain number of lemonade stands during a year, we will have to prove via documentation (perhaps notes, pictures, accurate records of materials used) that we fulfilled that commitment in order to maintain a positive status with our funder.

If we don't maintain those records and cannot prove that we did what we said we were going to, we risk our good standing with that funder. They may not fund any projects of ours in the future. In addition, word gets around when organizations aren't reliable or truthful. That one situation could affect our relationship with many potential funders. It is your responsibility to find out what exactly needs to be documented and how.

Motivations and Takeaways

- Good communication may be the single most important factor in raising your organization to the level of other well-run, profit-making businesses.

- Carefully consider each communication you make, taking into account that the best way to get your message across may be in person, over the phone, or electronically. Do not default to electronic communication.

- Always be prompt when returning others' messages, emails, etc.

- Keep your messages clear and concise, consistent in tone, well-written grammatically, and spelled correctly. Proofread to make sure this is the case.

- Familiarize yourself with and use the vocabulary of your given industry or geographic area as well as common business terms. This assists in your credibility as an organization.

- Document everything.

CHAPTER 12

Keys to Success
Effectiveness, Efficiency, and Flexibility

*Some corporations are extremely well managed;
some nonprofits are. It has nothing to do with
the sector. It has to do with the quality of
management.*

—FRANCES HESSELBEIN

In this book, we've looked at the similarities between nonprofit and for-profit organizations, and spoken to the value of nonprofits looking to best business practices from the for-profit world. But there are key differences between the two, beyond the obvious distinction that one makes a profit for its people, and the other makes money for its mission. One is in the way they actually operate, and one is the way in which the industries are perceived.

Briefly, nonprofits do operate, in many ways, differently than for-profit businesses do. They usually operate on tighter budgets (particularly smaller nonprofits), often have to get by with less manpower, and have challenges obtaining other resources. Because budgets are smaller, a few people often have to do the jobs of many, forcing some to wear multiple hats. This can lead to burnout very quickly in the nonprofit sector, not only because people are carrying large workloads (after all, people do that in corporate America all of the time) but also because nonprofit work is often emotionally taxing.

For-profit businesses generally have larger budgets and more resources, more manpower, the ability to provide competitive salaries and hire the best people, and better benefits. For-profit businesses often get to use the latest and greatest technology, and although corporate America may sometimes be seen as greedy, most for-profit companies are quick to respond to consumer demands and desires and can maintain a positive image as long as they do so.

With respect to how both sectors are perceived, think about this example. Corporation A, a for-profit corporation with national reach, has a large budget. Over 50 percent of that budget goes to overhead expenses, or expenses that are necessary to run the business, e.g., rent, electricity, and salaries, but no one complains that its overhead costs are too high. Nonprofit Organization A also has a national reach, several hundred employees, and a large budget (think the Red Cross or the American Cancer Society). Only 30 percent of its budget is dedicated to overhead expenses, but people criticize the organization for not spending enough on direct service or the cause they are helping. 60-some cents of every dollar donated to Nonprofit Organization A goes directly to the cause, but many, many people would look at that number and decide not to donate to that organization because they feel not enough of their donations go directly to service and outreach. Conversely, in order to provide its services, Nonprofit Organization A, just like Corporation A, must also maintain an office, pay for things like electricity and supplies, and pay its employees' salaries. How is Nonprofit Organization A supposed to run effectively and efficiently if it's supposed to lower its expenses even further?

These expectations of nonprofits (which are unrealistic, by the way) as well as challenges like the fact that some nonprofit executive directors make astronomical salaries, contribute to the public's misinformed perceptions of nonprofits. Just like for-profit companies, these perceptions can be good or bad. Some people see nonprofits as selfless, noble, and necessary, whereas others perceive them as constantly having their hand out, not using their resources wisely, and not being well-managed. Some people think nonprofits are easily and most likely funded by deep-pocket donors (which is almost never the case). These perceptions, among others, put nonprofits at a disadvantage from the start, which is a shame. Our society needs what the nonprofit sector provides, but in most cases, they want those services for less than even the for-profit sector could provide them for. So what do we do?

It's highly unlikely that we can change the entire public's perception of the nonprofit sector, but we can change some things in the industry. As the quote at the beginning of the chapter says, there are for-profits and nonprofits that are run well, and others that are run poorly. What we can do is demonstrate well-run nonprofits so that the perception of the sector is improved. That will require really using our heads.

How do we run nonprofits better? Well, if the for-profit world is doing it well, we should borrow from it. There is never a good reason to reinvent the wheel. If for-profit businesses are successful when they do certain things, let's learn from that. When they don't do those things, they go under. Both circumstances are informative for us. There's no reason why many of those things that work cannot and should not be translated to the nonprofit sector. Now, does that mean we get to do everything the way the for-profit sector does? Well, no, because we are generally running on fewer resources and putting our funds back into our organizations. We may have to be creative and adapt certain things. But there is so much the nonprofit sector can learn from the for-profit world about being efficient, effective, and simply smarter.

When Patti Donnelly first came to the Literacy Council of Northern Virginia (LCNV) as the executive director, she faced several challenges, but summed them up by this very idea. She said, "Beyond the first immediate concern of establishing some staff order and a functioning office environment, I faced a kind, but inexperienced board. Another initial challenge was the realization that 80 percent of the revenue was government grant-based, in a very volatile government funding environment. There was no individual fund-raising in place as the board was opposed to soliciting for gifts from its mailing list of volunteers. I guess most simply, with these two examples, my challenge was to change the culture of a grassroots-driven management structure and demonstrate to the board and volunteers that we were going to run this organization like a business."

Working Effectively:
Getting Things Done Well

So what kinds of things am I talking about? Some we've already discussed and aren't difficult, even though they may take time and preparation at the beginning of forming your organization. For example, for-profit businesses rely on content area experts for necessary tasks. Although not everyone in your organization has to be a content expert and many things can be learned, this echoes my original advice to pay for legal and accounting services. These are specialized areas in which most of us are not experts. They are also areas in which easily made mistakes can have dire consequences. Even when spending the money to get expert advice seems prohibitive, it's nonetheless worthwhile.

So is the act of using signed contracts or agreements, both internally and externally. Businesses operate on agreements signed by both parties that are benefitting from the services. Although it would be awesome to still live in a world where a handshake was as good as a signed contract, it's just not so anymore. Take the lead from for-profit businesses, and make sure everything from employees acknowledging all of your policies and procedures to partnership agreements with other organizations are signed. Though these may be called different things at times, such as letters of agreement or memorandums of understanding instead of contracts, they are just as important. Not only do they protect you legally, but they also make sure that all parties know up front what they're getting into.

I also urge you to learn the key basic skills you will need

as the director of an organization, which you will be until you choose to hire someone to do so. One of these is the ability to read basic financial reports. Although you will not need to know all of the intricacies of filing proper taxes and reconciling all of your statements and accounts, you will need a fundamental understanding of how to read a balance sheet, a cash flow statement, and various versions of budgets. Not only should you comprehend these things, but you should also make sure your staff does too. Everyone in the organization should have a cursory grasp of the financial side of the organization. This keeps everyone informed and aware of the organization's financial status and gives all staff, including those who may focus on programs or direct service, an idea of where funding comes from, how it is used, and where it goes, which allows everyone in the organization to be able to speak intelligently about the organization's finances.

Comprehension of financial issues is one area in which nonprofits often fall short. This could be for several reasons: people who begin nonprofits often don't have extensive business experience, one person often has to serve in multiple capacities, and there can be a false belief that not everyone needs to be aware of these things. If we want to be more efficient and effective as nonprofits, we can and must change this. We want to elevate everyone's understanding of business procedures so that our organizations can be taken more seriously. We want to project professionalism rather than the sense that we are just piecing things together as we go. As with most other things, the way to become more professional is through education.

Education in the area of finances and the metrics in which

your organization operates (number of people served, number of activities completed, etc.), not only elevates the professionalism of the organization but also gives employees, volunteers, and board members more buy-in, more interest in the organization. It gives them feelings of responsibility for and pride in their work.

President and Executive Director Donald Papson, of the M.S. Hershey Foundation, shares key numbers and metrics with his staff on a regular basis. It gives his employees at the Hershey Gardens, The Hershey Story Museum, and the Hershey Theater pride of ownership in their work. He cites needing employees who are not only dedicated to your mission but also dedicated to meeting metrics that are crucial to your success. "Although it takes time for some employees to get used to the numbers, gentle introductions, making it fun, and explaining how they can help drive attendance get employees excited, which contributes to a successful foundation," says Mr. Papson. For-profits do this all the time through meetings and memos and expectations that everyone be on the same page. If nonprofits are to become more successful, nonprofits should do this too.

Does this mean you have to do numbers exactly the way for-profits do? No. In fact, when you're starting out, financials will be a little less complicated. That's when it's a good time to familiarize anyone you bring on board with your desire for them to understand the numbers. This can simply mean going over your start-up budget and explaining each line to your new employee or board member. Share with them what things cost, what amount of money you expect to bring in, and where you expect it to come from. Discuss ways to save and ways to promote your services. Decide what types of numbers would help motivate them to do their jobs. For example, does it make more sense to them when you share with them the number of clients served or the monetary equivalent of the services you provided?

For LALO, we could count the number of people who visit our lemonade stands, the amount of money each stand brings in, the average donation, the number of things the donations were able to buy, or the number of children who were affected by donations. In some cases, it might make sense to capture all of those numbers and share them. In other cases, you won't need to share all of those numbers all of the time. Just remember, become intimately familiar with the numbers, share and expect others to, at the very least, have a cursory knowledge of them, and use them to help motivate and inform your employees and programs.

I've also discussed this previously, but it cannot be over-stated that having policies and procedures documented and shared with those in your organization is absolutely crucial. Yes, for- profit businesses often have more red tape to unwind than nonprofits do. However, much of that red tape was (at least initially) developed for a good reason, and businesses that consistently maintain their policies and procedures run smoothly. Employees, volunteers, and board members need to know what is expected of them and why. This does not mean your organization must be very authoritative or top-down in its management style. It simply means that there needs to be rules and everyone needs to be aware of them. These include hiring practices, job descriptions, vacation and sick policies, processes for employee evaluations and probationary periods, and even things as simple as dress codes. Policies can always be changed. As your organization evolves, you may find that things you developed at the beginning don't work anymore. Therefore, you should revisit policies and procedures and change them as necessary, but it is crucial to the efficiency and effectiveness of the organization to have these things developed from the start. This avoids questions, confusion, disagreements, and lots of wasted time.

I've made my own mistakes both in running programs and being an employee, and I can tell you from experience that working with an organization that has no policies and procedures in place may seem like fun, but it's really not. I once worked for a startup nonprofit that hired me through word of mouth to write grants. It was understood that I would work from home and write grant applications for funding as assigned—or for grants that I came across myself. However, there were no guidelines as to how vigorously I should look for grant opportunities versus how much I should rely on my supervisor to tell me which to apply for. There was no procedure for turning in my hours or being paid, so I was able to create my own invoices as an independent contractor. I should have asked right away for written clarification on these things, but I didn't. Big mistake because while all of this seems like a cushy position to be in, I eventually became extremely frustrated because unbeknownst to me, the organization brought on another colleague to also write grants. I was surprised because I hadn't been told that we needed to apply for more grants, that I wasn't applying for enough, or that I needed help. This person just kind of showed up, and it was my responsibility to get her up to speed.

171

At this point, I realized how important it was that I have a job description so that I knew exactly what I was responsible for versus what a second grant writer was responsible for. Without expectations of me laid out, things became kind of awkward. I began to feel confused and unappreciated. I wasn't receiving any feedback as to whether I should be doing more or less, whether my work was satisfactory or not, and how this new person and I were to collaborate.

On top of that, the process that seemed to be working was that I wrote the grants and the director submitted them. I assumed this was so the director had a chance to review things and submit them under her name. I continued with that process, not knowing it was a problem because I had never been told that it was. Suddenly, upon completing this process for what was the 10th or 12th time, I was told that the process caused too many headaches and complications, and I was to be doing the submissions and/or deliveries myself. That was fine with me, but what wasn't fine was that this had never been explained to me, and when it finally was, it was through an email to the entire staff rather than a conversation with me personally. I felt very called out, and eventually I got fed up and left, feeling very hurt. From an employee's point of view, you need to provide policies, procedures, and expectations to help keep your employees focused, content, and clear on their responsibilities.

Not only do you want things outlined for your employees, but you also want to make sure you have policies and procedures in place for volunteers, including vetting them properly. Just as you will go through a hiring process for paid employees, you should go through a similar process with volunteers. For-profit companies vet employees in fairly substantial ways, including applications and resumes, multiple interviews, and criminal background checks. Although you do not always have to go to those lengths (unless you work with minors—make sure you research policies having to do with background checks for those having contact with children) to scrutinize possible volunteers, it's important to make sure that you're not only a fit for the volunteer, but that the volunteer is a fit for you.

Volunteers will be interested in different tasks, and different tasks will require different skillsets. There will be opportunities in which a volunteer's personality is very important, and others in which volunteers may be working mostly alone. Some volunteers may be willing to collaborate, and others might not. Some will be looking for opportunities to manage others, and some will simply want to offer their hours. Knowing these things ahead of time is crucial to deciding whether a volunteer is a good fit for your organization. Just as you would with employees, look for qualified volunteers, and give them specific roles to fulfill. Be consistent and kind in your policies, and think ahead. You don't want to have to work as hard as I did to get a Mr. and Mrs. Smith to respect and cooperate with you (refer back to Chapter 9).

Working Efficiently: Getting Things Done Without Wasting Resources

Running Meetings

Another key skill that every leader in the nonprofit industry should master is how to run an efficient and effective meeting. If you've never sat through a wretchedly boring, drawn-out, time- wasting meeting, consider yourself lucky. And just because you don't have a cushy corporate office or a conference room with catered snacks does not mean you can't run a professional meeting. I referred briefly to Robert's Rules of Order earlier (Chapter 7). Though some of the steps in these meeting procedures might not be necessary for your organization, they provide a structure for meetings that can help you start out on good footing and stay on track. They equip you with the proper way to vote on things, proceed from one item to another, and maintain professionalism. Here are some other secrets about the best ways to run a meeting that Robert's Rules of Order doesn't tell you:

Always have an agenda and stick to it. This will most likely be the responsibility of the board chairperson, although you may need to take on this responsibility at first. Have someone else put eyes on the agenda to make sure you haven't made grammatical or spelling errors and to see if there is anything you've forgotten. In addition, once you have formed a board of several people, send a draft agenda to your meeting attendees prior to the meeting so they can add things if needed and feel prepared. When creating the agenda, include who will be speaking about which item and how long the group should spend on that item. For example, A) Program Summary—7:10–7:30 p.m.—Jill

Work with the board chairperson to move smoothly from each agenda item on the list to another, citing given time limits. If you have trouble getting through a certain topic, allow more time at the next meeting or adjust the order of the meeting so that necessary business decisions are made first and things requiring lots of discussion come later.

Have someone (eventually, the board secretary) take detailed notes or minutes of the meeting. These should be cleaned up and sent to the group as soon as possible after the meeting is over so that the group can check for any mistakes or things that were left out, and so everyone knows their responsibilities and action items that came out of the meeting. This is the only way people will be held accountable for what they say they are going to do. It also informs your agenda for your next meeting, as you know what you need to revisit and cover.

Do not let anyone hijack the meeting! I know, a little harsh, right? What I mean to say is that sometimes there are people who very much enjoy hearing their own voices. They may have strong opinions, or simply be lonely or need human interaction. Some of those people may be on your board, but it's important that no one person seizes control of the agenda. There are several ways to deal with this, including limiting discussion of each agenda item to a certain amount of time (thus the time limits on your agenda). You can also gently remind the group that everyone needs to have a chance to speak, that you are all attending for the good of the organization, and that everyone has valuable input. Finally, a simple, "We're going to move on from that item now," can help.

Stick to the time limits of your meetings. In other words, if you plan your meeting for 7-8 p.m., make sure you adjourn as close to 8 p.m. as possible. This shows respect for everyone's time and effort, and it encourages people to maintain their presence. When people know that they will be at a meeting for a specified amount of time and that time will be consistently honored, they will be more willing participants.

Community Engagement

Finding and making partnerships with other organizations is also an integral key to success. For-profit companies build relationships with other businesses all the time. They outsource certain tasks to companies that specialize in them, they collaborate with other businesses on large projects, and they often partner with nonprofit organizations to provide community service. Public-private-nonprofit sector partnerships are a growing area of collaboration. Not only can these partnerships help increase efficiency but they can also be a way to study your changing market and assess your needs to determine growth or strategic direction. Capitalizing on the resources and knowledge partners have is very smart and beneficial to both parties.

It's also tremendously important to find other nonprofit organizations you can partner with such that you can help each other. If you need assistance with technology, for example, it would be great to find an organization that does that well and could give you some pointers. In return, you could offer them services that you do well. Maybe you have developed a great record-keeping system for volunteers, or perhaps you had to develop a program from scratch that could be used as an example for another organization. Maybe you decide to partner with another agency to write a grant application that would provide funding for both of you. Granting organizations love collaboration because it shows willingness to work together to benefit the community as well as a good way to leverage funding and work to both organizations' strengths.

Learn about your local community and local businesses and organizations that could support you in different ways. Be an integral part of the community by showing up at community events and getting the word out about your organization. Always be willing to network with others, sharing your story and listening to the stories they have to share. Building these relationships can lead to partnerships and collaborations you never knew were possible.

Public Relations

Another thing the for-profit sector does well is public relations. For-profit businesses have become very good at crafting their messages to appeal to their audiences. They are good at marketing their services and products, and they are also good at using the media to their advantage. As a nonprofit, you will still need to market your organization even though it's fulfilling a need in the community. Just because people need what you're offering does not mean they will unconsciously become aware of what you're doing or simply approach you for it. You're going to have to be smart and strategic with your outreach, as it's called in the nonprofit sector.

Think back to Chapter 7, when we talked about networking. This is very similar. You are going to have to brainstorm to determine who needs to hear what you do and how best they will receive it. If you're offering a food program, for example, will you be offering it to clients who are asking for help or those who are embarrassed to ask? You will have to communicate your message where they will be able to find it—schools, churches, social services offices. If you're providing a program or service for children, you're going to have to target their parents with your message because, after all, it's those parents who provide transportation, finances, and permission for their children to participate in programs and activities.

For LALO, we have a heart-tugging cause—children who are suffering. Although that will make for an easy request for donations, we must still communicate clearly how we are going to help those children, since there are tons of charities out there for kids. We'll have to make sure we share that we're providing comfort and care to children staying in the hospital for treatments rather than sending money to research or to something like the Ronald McDonald house. And that will determine where we should share our message. Here, as above, we'd likely target schools, churches, community centers, after-school programs, etc.

Nonprofits often underestimate their power to present a professional message. Even though nonprofits don't often have the budgets for marketing materials that for-profits do, it is sometimes prudent to spend some extra money for professional-looking promotional items like newsletters or annual reports. These days, it's easy to produce some nice-looking newsletters with graphics and photos on simple computer programs. That's very beneficial to nonprofits working on small budgets.

There are other times when you will want to step up your game and really demonstrate how competent and committed you are to your cause. For example, an annual report, with a glossy cover and clear photos, is a good thing to put a little more money into so that it can act and look like those from the for-profit world. Something like an annual report gets sent to so many donors, stakeholders, and potential investors that it's worth spending a little extra money for the professionalism of an outsourced, printed item. It's always worth weighing the financial burden of these decisions, but it's important to note that in some cases, particularly when you're marketing your organization, you want to put your best foot forward, projecting as much professionalism as possible. The respect it garners you will be invaluable in the future.

Many nonprofit professionals are uneasy or unfamiliar with the use of the media for outreach and resources. No need to be afraid! You'll find that most staff of newspapers, radio stations, and local news channels are very receptive to assisting nonprofits, and can be a tremendous help in getting your message out there. Again, as in Chapter 7, the best way to make these connections is personally. Everyone has an email address and social media accounts, but you'll get much further by making a personal connection. If you prefer, a first contact through email or website is fine as long as you are sure to follow up over the phone. Try to find out the best time to reach the people you're looking for. In the local news media, for example, the best time to reach reporters and anchors at their desks is mid to late morning, after they've had their morning meeting. Don't be afraid to make requests, ask for assistance, or ask for donations or services for free. Do remember to be courteous, considerate of their time, and appreciative. It always pays to send a handwritten note or email thanking anyone in the media who has assisted you in some way. Those small gestures go a long way in forming lasting relationships.

Flexibility

In the nonprofit industry, flexibility can mean the difference between life and death. Not for people, mind you, but for your organization. And for once, this is one area in which the nonprofit sector could teach the for-profit sector a thing or two—yay! No one knows how to be more flexible than a grassroots, nonprofit employee who manages programs, enters data, serves as the IT person, and also cleans out the office refrigerator. Serving in many roles is as inherent in the nonprofit world as going with the flow—the flow of community needs, the flow of people power, and the flow of money. With our society constantly changing, people and funding come and go like the soup of the day at your favorite restaurant. Nonprofits must be willing to try new things, be open to new ideas, and not get stuck in old habits. Nonprofits must master the ability to adapt on short notice so they can survive the ever-changing economy and social landscape.

At the Literacy Council of Northern Virginia, a change in programming direction was precipitated by changes in funding focuses and goals. Its founding tutoring program met learners where they were in their learning and provided one-to-one instruction to personalize the process without the shame of not knowing how to read. It also gave volunteers a great way to build relationships. But as the learning landscape changed and more learners needed English language skills and job skills, LCNV had to decide to make a program shift. Its new program, Destination Workforce, grew out of the need to get its learners where they needed to go faster and smarter. The goal or purpose became to advance professionally, whether that was simply getting any job or moving up professionally. Tutoring one-hour per week was a great way to learn but it took a long time to make educational gains, whereas a workplace-focused class that meets for two hours, three times a week, framed in a targeted industry, where learners can get a professional credential, was going to make a difference in job attainment or advancement within a year. For LCNV, the ideal model of this looked like working in partnership with businesses with existing entry-level service staff—in one case, the hospitality industry. Holding classes at the hotel between shifts, the curriculum is written to accommodate language and procedures within the service sector (like housekeeping or back-kitchen), and what the credentialed learners receive is the Gold Star Customer Service certificate.

This chapter relates in many ways to the final chapter in the book, which discusses common mistakes and pitfalls. As you can tell from the topics in this chapter, it doesn't take much to turn these recommendations from the for-profit sector on their head to envision potential pitfalls. But we'll revisit some of them in the upcoming pages.

Motivations and Takeaways

- In order to be successful in the nonprofit sector, you must run your organization like a business. Borrow common practices from the for-profit sector to expand your effectiveness and efficiency.
- Hire professionals when you need them.
  They're worth it.
- Make sure you have signed agreements for every

partnership as well as with all of your employees, volunteers, and board members.

- Know your finance numbers and make sure your employees know them too!

- Have written policies, procedures, and job descriptions, and use them.

- Vet your volunteers and make sure they are matched with the right job so that the placement is successful for you and for them.

- Run effective meetings, use agendas and minutes, time limits on agenda items, and Roberts' Rules of Order to run meetings.

- Form partnerships with other people and organizations that will work to everyone's benefit.

- Make sure you have a professional message to use in outreach and marketing, and learn how to use the media to your advantage.

- Be flexible and willing to adapt and respond to changes in funding and community needs.

CHAPTER 13

Scary Stuff

Change, Growth, and Risk

Change is the only constant.

—HERACLITUS

We've already covered many of the challenges you might face when starting this journey. It's unfortunate that I can't promise you the challenges will be limited to the beginning stages of creating this organization. As you develop your organization, build it, and grow it, challenges will continue to arise. Most of these will arise organically, so it can be difficult to predict and therefore deal with change, growth, and risk tolerance ahead of time. That said, there are things I can tell you that might help!

Change

The Greek philosopher Heraclitus coined the phrase, "Change is the only constant." Simply as a human, you know this to be true. If you're a human parent, you live this every day. I mean, I can't tell you the number of times I've settled into whatever phase my kids were going through, thinking I finally had a handle on this parenting thing, and suddenly BAM! Totally new stage, new behaviors, and new things I haven't figured out. Yes, change is never-ending, and it will be for your organization as well. But the good news is that you can handle it.

Change will occur almost from the very beginning. You will think you're going down one path when suddenly, you'll be headed somewhere else. You'll expect a certain outcome when a different one will come totally from left field. You'll map out a plan and, at some point, there will be a hitch. Most changes come unexpectedly, which makes them difficult to anticipate and prepare for. There are others we can usually see on the horizon. For example, it's safe to assume that changes in funding, personnel, and external conditions will be almost constant. (It's not safe to assume anything else … after all, the word assume breaks down in tongue-in-cheek fashion to making "an ass out of you and me.")

What can you do to be ready for these changes? Several things, actually. Number one, having policies and procedures in place for personnel is key. You will want your employees to give you a certain amount of required notice before they go to an appointment, go on vacation, and even leave the organization. You'll want to have regular evaluations to determine if everyone is performing well. You'll want to spell out your expectations and make everyone aware of them so that no one can be surprised. As for funding, you'll want to have multiple funding streams so that should one grant run out or one large donor fail to donate again, you will have other funds on which to rely. You'll want to stay aware of the external environment—are there new organizations trying to break in and do what you're doing? Is there no longer a need for what you offer? Are you working yourself out of a job?

Not only you but also everyone else in the organization needs to get used to change. When a group of people coalesce around an idea or an event or an organization, it's very easy to get stuck in the pattern of, "But we've always done it this way!" Don't let that happen to you and your employees. While it's great to have organizational history and employees or volunteers or board members who have been around since the beginning and can share a historical perspective, you have to continually be forward-thinking. Perhaps something that you've done the same way for three or four years still works. Great! But perhaps it doesn't. Perhaps there's a better way out there to do it. Maybe you've done some research or talked to people from another organization. Perhaps you've brought on a new employee who has a fresh look at what you're doing and how you're doing it. Everyone in the organization must be open not only to listening to new ideas and new ways of doing things but also trying them out.

I once heard a story about a woman who learned how to bake a ham from her mother. Every time her mother baked a ham, she cut part of the end off before putting it in the oven. As she was growing up, the woman noticed this and began doing this herself as she began cooking for her own family. Well, her daughter watched and learned the same trick. But at one point the daughter (also the granddaughter), decided to ask her mother why she did it that way. Her mother told her it was because her mother did it that way. So, the granddaughter asked her grandmother why she did it that way. The grandmother replied, "Because the ham wouldn't fit in my oven!"

That story always gives me a little chuckle because we tend to assume that because something is done one way, it should always be done that way. However, we often don't know the origin of the reason for something, and often times that reason is no longer valid. Here the granddaughter and her mother had been throwing away good pieces of ham all along when they could have easily fit the ham into their newer, larger ovens! Simply put, there is nothing to be gained from staying stagnant, and there's nothing to lose when trying something new. Even if that new thing doesn't work and you have to change again or revert to a previous process, there's no shame in that. Don't let your organization fear change. It can be amazing!

Do you remember the term groupthink from Chapter 7? Groupthink is an organizational psychology term that warns us against getting swept up into going with the group consensus all of the time. This too can be an obstacle to change to be aware of, particularly if you have some change-resistors in your organization or on your board. Others might be afraid to suggest or accept change because the people who resist can be forceful or influential. However, encouraging everyone to provide their perspectives is key. If someone is uncomfortable sharing in a group of employees or volunteers or board members, it's ok to allow them to speak to you privately. It's important that everyone has a chance to weigh in on things or propose new ideas without fear of criticism. It's equally as important for those who oppose a new idea to be able to be heard. In other words, make sure you create an environment in which everyone is encouraged to share new ideas and where everyone is equally safe in straying from the group's opinion when they feel necessary. As I cited earlier, CINCH (Coalition for Infant and Child Health) in Norfolk, Virginia, is a consistently positive example of how to handle change well. Though the organization has a fiscal sponsor through Eastern Virginia Medical School, most of its programs are funded by grants—and the only constant about grants is that they change. One grant is always ending while another one is beginning; you're searching for new grants while in the middle of the hard work of others. It's challenging to be reliant on grant funding, one reason being because each grant is different and requires different activities and even different programs. For an organization like CINCH that focuses on the larger area of children's health, this works out most of the time. It also means constantly developing new programs and ways to address local health issues.

This was true in a big way in 2009 when a large children's health insurance recruitment program funded by the state government came to an end. The director not only had to brainstorm in which direction the organization would direct its efforts next but also had to decide what to do with the employees who had been grant-funded by that program. Luckily, it worked out for CINCH, as some people decided to voluntarily leave the organization and some were assigned to other grant-funded projects. In addition, CINCH dedicated its now available time and resources to expanding one of its other workgroups, one addressing Health Disparities. CINCH has been able to demonstrate time and again how adaptable it is not only to changing funding but also to changing community needs.

Growth

One of your biggest changes will be growth. Growth is a fantastic double-edged sword. Growth is wonderful for your organization, something you strive for and hope for. Growth is also a big challenge, since it brings greater demand for your services, increased need for manpower, increased need for funding, and, subsequently, increased things to do like managing more people and programs. Growing pains can be real, especially in the early stages when there are no clear instructions directing you down a specific path. What's worked for one organization may not work for you, and so you may have to forge your own path.

One of the most important things to note about growth is that it is very easy to begin to stray from your mission as you begin to grow. This "mission drift," as it's called, means wandering from your original intended aims and goals. More formally, straying from your intended mission. This happens because growing is so new and exciting that it can be tempting to grow for the sake of growing rather than for the sake of the mission of the organization. After all, bigger usually means more publicity, more public awareness, and even more recognition, which can be very ego-boosting, energizing, and even addicting. You might even find that you come to love recognition and praise more than you love doing the actual work of the organization.

Many leaders in many sectors get swept up in the excitement

of being well-known and even sought out. Keep in mind that if this becomes true for you, you might end up putting your desire for fame ahead of the goals of the organization, in which case you need to decide whether your true motivation is for personal or organizational gain. There's nothing wrong with personal gain, but it can sometimes stand in the way of your nonprofit actually doing its needed work. If that situation arises, you will have to make a decision for the good of the organization whether you want to pursue personal acknowledgement as your primary goal or the work of the organization. Keep in mind the two are not mutually exclusive, but they must be in balance with one another.

In contemplating any type of growth, the most important thing to ask yourself is whether or not that growth would be in line with your mission. Professor of Management Tammy Hiller of Bucknell University says, "Research on nonprofit organizations shows that mission drift is a big contribution to failure. One way to help alleviate this is to establish some rules or norms around decision-making to help make difficult choices."

For example, if you want to feed children after school and have the opportunity to grow into new areas, you'll want those areas to be relevant. It would make sense for you to expand into possibly feeding children at other times or sending food home with them. It would not make sense for you to expand into unrelated areas such as providing medical services or building homes. There are most likely other organizations who already do that. For LALO, this might mean we expand our offerings to include more than lemonade, that we expand to assist additional children's hospitals, or that we decide to expand from the Child Life Program into something for, say, siblings of hospitalized children. It would not be prudent for us to expand into something like tutoring after school or doing food collections for local food banks.

I've seen this play out many times in real nonprofits. One of the most glaring examples of this happened in a medium-sized local nonprofit. This particular nonprofit focuses on different areas of charity, including adoption, foster care, immigration and refugee services, and teaching English as a Second Language to immigrants. The organization also owns a large parcel of land on which a specialized school that serves children with behavior problems stands. The school needs to be renovated, and it's not bringing in the money to do so. The rest of the land is currently being leased to a local farmer, but for a very small amount of money. In fact, the amount is so small that even the farmer thinks he should be charged more! So, the debate is what to do with the rest of the land, which is many acres. The board of the organization has discussed this at length, and several ideas came up, including the idea of a solar farm. Some research was done, and indeed the land is perfect for a solar farm. Believe it or not, it's not the idea of a solar farm that worries me, even though that doesn't underscore the organization's mission. It's what follows next that sent me into a tailspin.

There are two options. The first option is to lease the land to a solar farm company who would do all of the work and maintenance and sell the energy back to the electric company. The solar farm company would then pay a straight $250,000 a year to this organization for the land. So all in all, easy $250,000 annually with little to no work. Great. The second option is for the organization itself to take charge of building and maintaining the solar farm. Now if you'll remember, this organization has zero experience in the solar industry, and its mission is to serve families in need in its local community.

To me, this is a no brainer. The organization has no expertise, no experience, and no knowledge of solar farming. I would vote for outsourcing the land to a solar farming company and simply collecting the lease money, which can then be used for the school. Let me be clear—no good can come of this organization entering into the solar farming business itself. Number one, solar farming has absolutely nothing to do with its mission. Number two, no one in the organization has any expertise in this area, and it wouldn't be prudent to bring someone on board simply for this reason because that would mean siphoning resources away from activities that fulfill the organization's mission. Finally, the board and staff of the organization are already wasting time and effort and subsequently money, on this decision. Any time a large decision like this is made, it takes time to go through all of the correct channels. There is no reason to spend time even debating this idea, as it has nothing to do with the mission of the organization. In plain words, running a solar farm (and we're not talking about abandoning the idea altogether— simply that the organization would hire a company to do it, not do it themselves), is not a good use of time or resources, nor does it make any sense.

There are some ways to avoid lost time on decisions like these. When developing policies and procedures with your board, it makes sense to either develop some criteria by which all decisions are measured or develop a process by which the board determines what kind of activities would indicate mission drift. For example, we could create some criteria for LALO about how we determine whether new projects would fit our mission. We could ask questions when new program ideas come up like:

- Does this idea or activity have to do with children who are hospitalized for long periods of time?

- Does this idea or activity have to do with raising money for hospitalized children?

- Does this new program or project provide revenue that would allow us to expand our reach to hospitalized children without using our necessary time and resources?

- Do we have expertise in this new idea or activity?

There are other questions you could create to determine whether you're staying true to your mission. You could even create a flow chart of yes/no questions to determine relation to your mission. Your board could work as a group on these decisions or a smaller group of employees and board members could assess these decisions themselves. You can also look outside your organization for opinions on whether an idea seems to be in line with your goals. There are lots of ways to put parameters around these decisions so that you don't end up straying from what you set out to do. The important thing is to be aware of possible mission drift, discuss it regularly when looking at expansion, and carefully and critically determine the right path for you.

Risk

Risk is inherent in deciding to start an organization, and it will be ongoing as you and your board manage your organization. Considering your level of exposure to injury or loss at every turn will become routine, but it doesn't have to be overwhelming. If you consider your SWOT analysis, you're already assessing and thinking about what risks the organization faces in all areas including programming, funding, employees and volunteers, and even facilities. Of course there are ways to mitigate risk, and the most common is insurance. You will need liability and property insurance, workers' compensation insurance, and possibly additional insurance for your volunteers as workers' compensation does not necessarily cover on-the-job injuries for volunteers (you'll have to check with your insurance company and your lawyer). You will also want to consult your lawyer about the necessity of insurance that covers direct contact with clients, especially children or other vulnerable populations, professional services like medical services (if you provide services that involve a potential risk), and even creating or publishing materials. You'll want to make sure your property and liability insurances cover the organization for special events that might take place off-site, damage to equipment or property you own or lease, and employee dishonesty (to protect against things like embezzlement). The organization might also need Directors and Officers insurance to protect the board members', officers', and employees' personal assets from lawsuits against the organization (which you will hopefully never face). Insurance professionals and lawyers can give you explicit guidance in this area, but it's always good to get a general idea of what you might need.

When it comes to protecting against risk for things like programs, services, and growth of the organization, there are things you can do. Again, reviewing your SWOT analysis and making continual assessments of the outside environment allow you to be aware of what's going on around you and plan for potential changes. When it comes to the programs or services you want to provide and whether you should expand or grow, it's important to have conversations about how much risk you're willing to take. Board members can be invaluable in these discussions because of their differing perspectives and areas of expertise. Some organizations have discussions about potential growth and its risk and go from there. Others take a more measured approach by assigning levels of risk to certain activities and then deciding at what levels they're willing to accept the risk and at what levels they're not willing to accept the risk. You will also hear the terms cost-benefit analysis when discussing risk. This refers to the costs to the organization for implementing certain things, risk being included, and what the organization will be getting out of implementing this certain thing, the benefits.

A good risk resource is the Nonprofit Risk Management Center. They have a wealth of articles, apps, conferences, and even consulting services. One particularly helpful article gives a good overview of risk and how your board should provide most of the oversight of risk the organization is willing to take. Check out The Garden of Risk Oversight: Positioning the Board to Cultivate Strategic Risk-Taking at the

Nonprofit Risk website for some tips.[15] Your decisions about risk, whether they are in regard to starting a new program, ending an old program, taking on new staff, or applying for a big grant, will, among other things, ultimately come down to how much risk your organization is comfortable with and willing to take.

This Is My Brave, Inc., is a mental health nonprofit based out of Northern Virginia. It was founded by two women, one of whom was diagnosed with Bipolar Disorder at the age of 26 while pursuing a successful career in recruiting. She had no prior experience with mental illness and suffered through several hospitalizations, manic, and depressive episodes before she found a successful treatment plan. As she was going through that experience, she began blogging and received a huge, supportive response. When she realized how many people had similar stories, she came up with the idea for a theater show in which people living successful lives with mental illnesses get up on stage and tell their stories creatively through original songs, poetry, and essays. She found a partner, and they mounted an inaugural show, then followed that by forming a nonprofit.

The decision to form This Is My Brave was a risky one. No one had ever put together something like this in the mental health arena. In addition, those with mental illness still face stigma, as our society has not yet chosen to fully educate itself and dispel rumors around mental illnesses. In addition, it was a risky prospect to assume that other people facing similar situations would want to tell their stories live in front of an audience. Luckily for the co-founders, This Is My Brave took off. The organization had such a positive response to its first show that it recognized the need to expand and do so rather quickly. Soon, one show became two, four, six, and even 10 shows across the country.

Growth for This Is My Brave (TIMB) was just as risky, if not more so, than its humble beginnings as a simple Kickstarter campaign. In order for TIMB to expand, it had to form a model that relied on volunteers to produce shows across the country. Volunteer producers had to do everything from hold auditions and choose cast members, to find venues, hold rehearsals, and fundraise for the production.

In addition, mental illness can be a sensitive and emotional subject to deal with, and often producers have to deal delicately with people's stories. This put a lot of responsibility on the shoulders of volunteers who the organization had, for the majority, never met in person. As each volunteer produced a new show in a new city, the organization realized what parameters it needed to add for volunteers who were doing this solely for the purpose of helping the organization. Even though the majority of volunteers had the best intentions, the organization still had to trust them to select the best stories, be kind with those who auditioned, recruit an audience, and make money that all got sent back to the organization.

Seemingly, a lot could go wrong in this scenario. There was no other way to expand, since the organization was small and didn't have the manpower or financial resources to staff every show everywhere. So, the organization put systems in place to try to foresee potential missteps and avoid them if possible, not only for the sake of the organization but also for the volunteers, as it was imperative this was a good experience for them as well.

While volunteers were given guidelines on how to produce shows, each time a new show was produced, the instructions, or "playbook," was updated with new scenarios, new guidelines, and new suggestions. In addition, more checks and balances were put in place as the organization grew to help determine the most qualified volunteers and safeguard things like liability and fundraising.

Volunteers were taught how to better use the fundraising platform, how to approach businesses for donations, and how to use the media to their advantage.

Today, This Is My Brave, Inc., is an international organization continuing to address the stigma around mental illness through its live shows it then posts to YouTube. It has struggled through the same growing pains other startup nonprofits do, and continues to overcome challenges as it expands. What it's done has been ground-breaking and very risky not only in its focus area but also in its use of resources, mostly volunteers. This Is My Brave's Executive Director and co- founder, Jennifer Marshall, has been featured in media outlets around the country, has spoken to national audiences, and continues her quest to make talking about mental illness just as common as talking about the weather.

Succession

Once you've built a successful, growing nonprofit, you will need to start thinking about its future. That might seem nonsensical at first because you're just starting out, and you may hope and plan to be there for the life of the organization. Or, you may be planning to solve the problem you want to solve and work yourself out of a job. Those are great goals, and they could happen. Life also happens—circumstances change, hurdles arise, and you need to think ahead. There may come a time when you decide you'd like to leave the organization or can no longer lead.

There are only two ways for you to move on from your organization. You can choose to leave the organization and allow it to go on, or you can choose to close the doors to your organization and distribute its assets to other organizations fulfilling a similar mission. Because no one person or group owns a nonprofit organization, if and when you choose to leave, you must leave the managing of it to someone else. Who is that going to be, and how are you going to feel about it?

Being the founder of any organization can be an emotional experience. You've invested your time and effort in building something from scratch, and you most likely made sacrifices in other areas of your life in order to fulfill this dream. It's not as easy as simply deciding that you're done. Some have even compared starting a nonprofit to birthing a baby—it's something that's a dream, that's in the planning stages for a long time, and, when it finally happens, it is miraculous and amazing and scary and surprising all at the same time. Not only have you started something, but you have also watched it grow, helped it develop, and seen it at its best and worst. It makes sense that any decision on how to move you or your organization forward can be difficult and emotional. Given all of these things, there's no doubt you want to leave your organization in good hands.

You want someone to lead it who has the same desire for it to succeed as you do and has a similar passion for its mission.

You also want someone who is competent, can follow through with plans that may already be in motion, and can envision a solid future for the organization. You need someone who can gel with your board and staff and whose personality would be a welcome addition to the team. Inevitably, no one will do things exactly the way you do them, and that can be hard to accept. But you may also find someone who has amazing ideas you hadn't thought of, ways to grow the organization that you couldn't have imagined, and a vision that includes things you never thought possible. In fact, your successor's vision may end up being very different from yours, but that's something you have to be prepared for when you begin an organization.

Although change, growth, and risk can be scary, they are inevitable. However, with proper planning and good resources like great employees and board members, they can be very positive for the organization. It's important to have a good imagination and positive attitude with a realistic look toward the future.

Motivations and Takeaways

- Change is the only constant. Be willing to sit with the uncomfortable feeling that things will always be changing.

- Growth is a double-edged sword. Growth can be both rewarding and challenging. Be sure you are growing in a way that supports your mission, and watch out for becoming addicted to the idea of growing for the attention and notoriety that it brings you or your organization.

- Risk is inherent in starting any organization. Use your staff, volunteers, and board to make sound decisions about risks for the organization.

- Though it's counterintuitive, keep succession in mind as early as you start forming your organization so you get used to the idea you will eventually have to turn over your organization to someone else or close its doors.

CHAPTER 14

Building Support
and Avoiding Burnout

When the well's dry, we know the worth of water.
—BENJAMIN FRANKLIN

Working in a nonprofit can be exhausting. Running one can be downright draining. One day you're talking strategy and funding and big plans, and the next you're sweeping the office floor. One minute things are going along swimmingly, and then you find out an employee or volunteer won't be showing up to provide services to your clients, so you have to fill in rather than spend time writing a grant proposal or building relationships with donors.

So how do you make sure that you don't burn out? You have the best intentions—to serve others, to solve a problem, to make the world a better place. But how do you continue that mentally and emotionally taxing work without depleting yourself? It is indeed no small task, but it can be done.

The primary way to preserve your own wellbeing is by

building a strong support system, both professionally and personally. This begins with building your organization with the right people, not only for the jobs they need to do but also for the sake of the entire team. You may find applicants who are qualified for the positions you have, but some may not be a good fit due to personality, ability to work with others, or ability to be a team player. You may find someone who just doesn't feel right or gel with you or your team. Trust your gut when it tells you that someone is just not a good fit for your organization. Be sure that the people you hire share your work ethic, your organization's values, and your passion for your mission. You want people who will have each other's backs, pitch in when someone needs a break, and respect their co-workers and leaders. This is never to say you should hire someone who fits these criteria but isn't qualified. This is simply to say you need to look for the best all-around candidates to join your team without one characteristic outweighing another. This will serve you well in the long run, particularly when things get difficult, tiresome, or tedious.

While hiring good people inside the organization is key, those people can only provide so much support to you as a leader. Having camaraderie and rapport with your employees and volunteers is not only healthy but also necessary. You need your own support system outside of your organization who can be there when you need a shoulder to cry on, an ear to vent to, or a squad to cheer you on and celebrate your milestones. For many of us, these support systems begin in our families, whether nuclear or extended. For others, families only bring added stress, and our true support systems lie within our friends. Either way, these people should be able to help and support you by being good listeners or sounding boards for your ideas and dreams. They should also be able to provide you with advice when and if you want it. Most of all, they should be there to support you when you need them most, whether that's to lend a hand at an organizational event, dry your tears, or take you out for a drink.

There are also people you can turn to in your own industry for help and support. Remember networking? This is another huge benefit. By making contacts throughout the nonprofit community, your geographic community, and the online community, you begin to build relationships. Growing and strengthening these relationships is key to your wellbeing as a nonprofit leader. There are colleagues all around who you can learn from, ask advice from, or simply talk to about common challenges and accomplishments. Other nonprofit and for-profit business leaders can be tremendous assets full of knowledge, wisdom, and connections. These relationships also build bridges for partnerships and collaborations.

Many nonprofit leaders find mentors in similar fields of business, and mentors are invaluable. Mentors can teach us the ins and outs of our business, connect us with others who can help us, and help us find the right paths. Look for a mentor through your own contacts, through your employees, volunteers, and board members, and through local business associations. SCORE (SCORE.org), which was previously known as the Service Corps of Retired Executives, is a nationwide network of over 11,0000 business mentors who are waiting to help you develop, manage, and grow your organization. SCORE is not only free but also has local chapters that offer free tools and cheap workshops and seminars. In addition to

SCORE, most metropolitan and suburban areas have many groups that can be more than worth joining, including Small Business Administration groups, your local chamber of commerce, and your local leadership group. These leadership groups are organizations throughout the country called "Leadership Name of City." For example, I would Google "Leadership Harrisburg" to find our local group. These organizations are a resource for businesses and community organizations that teach leadership skills and effective community service. They offer leadership courses and facilitate connections among the community.

It goes without saying that when you interact with other professionals, you should always be polite, willing to receive feedback and suggestions, and eager to learn. In addition, don't discount your own experience. Be willing to make yourself available to return the favor to anyone who asks you for advice or connections. After all, you may have an entire treasure trove of knowledge they don't have. And in the cases in which you have questions that need to be answered, do not be afraid to ask.

Other people can be a huge help in keeping you from burning out, but so can your own solid business structure and organizational policies. As we discussed earlier, start off with as much of your structures and policies in place as possible. The more work you do at the beginning, the easier things will be as you go. For example, it's a huge benefit to both you and your employees to create a policy to keep clear distinctions between work and non-work hours. Protect your personal time and that of your employees. Make sure that everyone knows when they are expected to be available and when they aren't, and adhere to those rules. In addition, if you or your employees need to work extra or unconventional hours for a special event, that's fine, but don't make it a practice. In the same way, be sure to have a solid vacation or personal leave policy and be sure you use it yourself. Everyone needs time away from work to replenish themselves. Remember the airplane story? You need to put on your own oxygen mask first before helping someone else with theirs. You must take care of yourself because if you are running on empty, you cannot be there for your employees or your mission. And as the leader, you are setting the example for your employees. Behave the way you want them to behave, including taking your own vacations and adhering to organization policies. Show them what taking care of yourself and avoiding burnout looks like.

In her book *Real. Big. Love.: A Difference Maker's Guide to Gain Greater Clarity, Energy, and Impact for Your Cause and Life,* Lisa Wade describes additional strategies to protect our service-minded souls from burning out. She acknowledges that our world is full of work to be done serving others, so much so that it's easy to become overwhelmed, especially when there's a lot to do but not enough people or resources to get it all done. This can make those of us who have the heart for the nonprofit sector feel stressed. For that reason, she developed the idea of Soulful Service, or serving from a place of authenticity (Real) and boldness (Big) driven by Love. Her concept is sustainable because: "In soulful service, we bring our full selves, our balanced selves, our happy selves, our whole selves to our service. We fill ourselves up so that we are not already depleted when we seek to offer help to a program, a cause, and especially to people. We serve from the overflow of our own fullness." So, we make sure that we are taking care of ourselves while we're taking care of others. Her recommendations for doing so include:

Do what makes your soul sing. In other words, finding your true passion. Don't just start a nonprofit because you feel like you should help a certain cause. Do it because you have the passion and the desire, and because it makes you happy. You will never be able to sustain your work or yourself if what you're doing doesn't make you happy. So here's a secret. If, at the end of this book, you come to the conclusion that getting this organization off the ground is not what makes your soul sing, that's ok. Running a nonprofit is tough work, and if you don't love it, it becomes that much harder. If you change your mind, I will still stand behind you and remain grateful that you read this book.

Make sure your values are reflected in your service. In all that you do in beginning and running this organization, be true to yourself, always. If something doesn't feel right to you, it probably isn't. Do not sacrifice your ethics and morals in the name of a good business decision. Not only will this keep you serving from a place of fullness, but it will also build your self-respect and the respect of others for you.

Love and care for yourself with the same compassion and commitment you serve others. You know how we talked about the fact that you already have the heart, the passion for this work and that's something I can't teach you? You have to take that same passion and turn it into compassion for yourself. While you're busy taking care of others, you must also take care of yourself with great love and care. What does this mean? It means taking care of your physical body and growing your mind. It means trusting your intuition, speaking your truth, and forgetting about what anyone else will think. It can also mean engaging in a spiritual practice that's meaningful for you, and/or my favorite, creating a daily gratitude practice.

I actually heard about this from a friend prior to reading Ms. Wade's book. It's proven to be one of the most influential and important routines I have in keeping myself focused and able to go out into the world and do the work I do. Each night, I take a post-it note and write down several things I am grateful for that day. Sometimes there are a couple, sometimes there are many. Sometimes they are simple—gratitude for green traffic lights or a day of sunshine; sometimes they are deeper—gratitude for a relationship, an opportunity, or the fact that my family and I are happy and healthy. It doesn't really matter what the notes say. The process of expressing gratitude is what's important.

This practice has changed my thought patterns such that I now go through my day with thoughts of gratitude in mind, debating what I will put on my notes. And because of that, there are usually too many to name. Each night, I fold those notes up and put them into a glass jar on my kitchen counter. At the end of the calendar year, I take time to read each of them and revisit all of those wonderful things that happened or made me feel grateful. It's a continuous process that helps keep a positive and realistic perspective, helps me stay thankful, and helps me stay connected to myself and others. It's a practice that could also be adapted for workplace use.

As your organization begins to grow, you will have to

consider how your employees and volunteers can avoid burnout as well. You can encourage them to take advantage of some of the above strategies, but you also have a responsibility to be an active part in preventing their burnout. One of the ways you can do this is to walk your talk. Like I said, you are the leader, and you need to set the tone in your organization. You need to set the example by doing things like taking your own vacation time and stepping away from your desk to take breaks when needed.

Recently, the Stanford Social Innovation Review published an article about the myths that perpetuate nonprofit burnout, and believing that nonprofit leaders have limited power is one of these myths. Author Ann-Sophie Morrissette says, "The most effective leaders in the nonprofit space are deeply mindful of how they move through the workplace and among their colleagues. They recognize the power they hold, and embrace their role as setting the example and setting the tone."[17]

Patti Donnelly experienced how much of an unknown influence she had on her staff when her best friend started to lose her battle with cancer. It had come as a shock to Patti when her friend's husband called the office one afternoon to ask her to come to the hospital, and Patti left the office upset. When she returned to work the next morning and asked how things had gone the rest of the previous afternoon, her employees told her the office was so quiet that they could have heard a pin drop. Several were in tears, and everyone felt the gravity of Patti's news. That was when Patti realized that though she didn't have to pretend that everything was great when it wasn't, her attitude, tone, and behavior had a significant impact on her employees' abilities to work effectively. She became more aware of how she moved through the workplace from then on.

Other myths cited in the article include the idea that many people think that paying employees more doesn't make much of a difference, but it does. This is a challenge for non-profits, but it can go a long way in keeping your employees happy and healthy because they are employees, after all, and not volunteers. In addition, it cited the importance of trying to make life easier for your employees (see ideas like bringing in breakfast or lunch once a month) and making sure that communication within the organization is as important as communication outside the organization. A final myth is the idea that many nonprofits should see their employees and volunteers as "family" in a rejection of typical corporate culture. This is harmful because nonprofit employees are professionals doing complex and highly demanding work. At the end of the day, everyone is committed to the mission of the organization, and blurring these relationship lines can lead to uncomfortable and awkward situations when someone needs to be evaluated or even let go.

Maintaining professional, respectful relationships will go a long way toward helping the culture of your organization and keeping employees from burning out.

Motivations and Takeaways

- Fatigue and burnout are real risks, particularly in nonprofit organizations. Create a support system all around you both personally and professionally

so you serve your organization from a place of
fullness, not emptiness.

- When building your organization, be strategic
  in hiring people and creating your policies and
  structures such that they support a work environment
  in which burnout is rare and unlikely rather than
  the norm.

- You are the nonprofit leader. You must act the part and
  set the tone for your organization. Set the example
  for your employees, and follow your own policies and
  procedures.

- Aim to support your employees by appreciating them
  through proper compensation, ways to make their
  lives easier, and appropriate professional relationships.

CHAPTER 15

Let Me Spare You the Pain
Common Pitfalls
and How to Avoid Them

A smart man makes a mistake, learns from it,
and never makes that mistake again.
But a wise man finds a smart man and learns
from him how to avoid the mistake altogether.

—ROY H. WILLIAMS

There's a lot that can go wrong when running any type of organization, and nonprofits are inherently challenging. But there's much you can do to avoid the most common pitfalls and worst- case scenarios. You have a lot more control than you think you do, and I can help you figure out where best to exercise it so that you avoid lots of pain and suffering. And, if you've read this book up to this point, you will realize that some of these points are very familiar, which underscores their importance.

Create policies and procedures, and use them from

the beginning. This is one of the easiest and most important messages you can get from this book. For-profit companies are successful because they have well-oiled systems in place for handling a multitude of scenarios that may arise. This begins with having basic policies and procedures for how you are going to run your organization. Build from the bottom up and inside out. Consider everything from how you would handle emergencies that arise to the mundane of how employees should dress. Spell job descriptions out clearly, make sure everyone knows what is expected of them, and create standardized guidelines for things like work hours, vacation, sick leave, time off, and even how you would like the phone answered. Nothing is too small to consider at the beginning. If you outgrow some policies, revise them. But getting it all down and starting off on the right foot is key.

Document everything. Second to having policies and procedures in place is the importance of documentation. It is imperative that you keep detailed, accurate records not only for accounting purposes but also when they relate to phone calls, client interactions, and personnel. It is not overkill to write down when you spoke to whom and regarding what. You do not need to record every minute of your day, but it is extremely helpful to have a running log of conversations, interactions with clients, and relationships with employees. This is particularly helpful when you run into sticky situations, whether inside of or outside of the organization. If an employee begins to consistently arrive late, which is against your policy, a written record of that cannot be disputed. You will then be able to show the employee in writing what has happened and why they might need to be disciplined (a policy you would already have in writing, of course). If a vendor promises you an order of something on a specific date, make note of that for later so if you don't receive what you were supposed to when you were supposed to, you have record of it. It is always better to over-document than find yourself with nothing to back up your story.

Use professionals when needed and pay them current market rates. Again, if you only are able to process a couple of messages from this book, please include this one. Professionals are professionals because they have gone through extensive schooling and training and have a great deal of experience. We all have important and useful gifts, but no one person can have every gift or be a professional in every subject. Do what you do best and hire the professionals to do the things that require special attention, like accounting and law, at the very least. There are just too many easy ways to get yourself in a jam by trying to accomplish these tasks alone. In addition, although you might find volunteers willing to do these things at first, it is still best practice to move to paid independent contractors for these tasks as they are complicated, require time, and need the attention of someone contracted to do it. Please, please hire an accountant and a lawyer.

Ask for help. Again, no one of us is an expert in everything, but there are lots of people out there who can steer you in the right direction. There is no shame in asking for help and/or collaborating with other people and organizations. The best leaders and managers rely on competent, knowledgeable employees to do the work they themselves are not equipped to do. You should not only make sure you have the right help in place within your organization but also be willing to seek outside advice and assistance when necessary. Look for a mentor, connect with those in your field, and look for support outside your field but in your community.

Do not rely on one revenue stream of any kind. You're going to need to find multiple funding sources, including bringing in money from your services, individual donations, corporate contributions, in-kind contributions, grants, and even fundraising campaigns and special events. Even within the fundraising category, be sure that you have a wide swath of funding sources so that a majority of your funding doesn't come from any one source, such as government grants. Remember that the financial landscape is constantly changing, so the more diversified you are in your funding, the more likely you are to survive the loss of one funding source at any time.

Use the expertise of someone who has experience in managing people. Running an organization becomes not just about operating a program or figuring out accounts payable or signing agreements. It's also about managing your people, whether they be employees or volunteers or both. You need to learn human resource and managerial tasks like setting policies and following through on them, learning to listen and receive feedback, and learning to evaluate people in order to help them do better for the organization. If you don't have this expertise, find someone who does and can either work with you or teach you how.

Speaking of people, namely employees, volunteers, and even people from other organizations, one tough lesson to learn is that **not everyone will follow through the way you're hoping they will.** You work hard and put your heart and soul into your work, but others may not. The co-founders of Someone To Tell It To found this to be disappointingly true. Michael Gingerich and Tom Kaden shared that, "...to constantly learn and relearn that not everyone does what they promise they will do nor is everyone who they tell you they are (and therefore disappoints us when they turn out to be someone different than we expected) is always a hard lesson to accept." It is always difficult to accept the shortcomings or even half-truths of others. That does not mean to say that you should always expect the worst. Still, it's beneficial to go in cautiously optimistic when you're embarking on a new relationship, asking for work to be done, or hoping someone else will develop the same passion you have for your mission.

Discern good, positive growth rather than biting off more than you can chew or getting caught up in becoming famous, so to speak. Growth is great for your organization, but it also must be done cautiously. You will encounter a multitude of opportunities to grow in different directions, but you have to decide which of those ways are appropriate for you and your organization. One path might sound really exciting and big and amazing and another might sound positive but not as thrilling. Make sure you're choosing the one that is best for the organization in the long run, one that is most in line with your mission. You have to be constantly aware of mission creep and watch out for opportunities like solar farms (Chapter 13) that could potentially derail you. Remember, this is about the mission of the organization you started, not you personally.

Don't be afraid. Don't be afraid to try something new, forge a new path, test a new product or program. You can always go back to what you were doing before if the new thing doesn't work out. But you're never going to know unless you try, which means you also have to let go of the fear of failure. You're taking a great risk by starting your organization to start with, so continue that spirit throughout its existence. If something doesn't work, try something else. There is no shame in making mistakes. There is only the thought of what could have been.

Do not let yourself or your team burn out. Make leave time and vacation policies and demonstrate the good example of using them. Build a team to support you as you support your organization. Reach out to others in the nonprofit and for-profit worlds for help and assistance. And finally, make sure to do what sustains you and what sustains your team.

Finally and most importantly, use both your head and your heart in this bold new endeavor. Although the passion for helping others, for making the world a better place, and for creating an organization that gives back is the strong heartbeat that drives you and keeps you going when it's gets hard, listen also to your head. Make smart business decisions because, quite simply, you can't help others and fulfill your mission without money. You need funding to fulfill your purpose just as any good business does—you simply choose to reinvest that money in your mission. So be sure to use your head as well, by borrowing successful practices from the for-profit world.

Since this chapter has been a running list of motivations and take-aways, I won't try to boil them down any further for you. There's no doubt this is a challenging adventure you've chosen to go on, but it's also going to be an incredible, inspiring, and affirming journey that you are now prepared for. I promise you that if you follow the recommendations in this book, you will not only avoid many, many headaches, and doses of ibuprofen, but you will also be equipped to establish a smart, well-run, successful, and compassionate nonprofit. And maybe you'll have fun doing it!

Conclusion

T hroughout my nonprofit career, my hero grandfather continued to support me. I still think in the back of his mind, he thought I was capable of more. Perhaps he simply thought that I should be running a nonprofit instead of working for one. And who knows? The possibilities are endless, and I am still young (well, not THAT young...). But I like to think that my grandfather would be very proud of me today because it's been in recent years that I have come to realize what he truly meant. Through my work with several startup nonprofits, being on the front lines of how things get started and grow, I've come to realize the importance of the business principles of the for-profit sector to the nonprofit sector. I've seen the link between the two, how they can both make a difference, and how they both need each other. I've learned they are not mutually exclusive but need to be complementary. Whereas before I thought they needed to be two very distinct entities, now I know the advantages of overlap and collaboration. In his heart of hearts, I think that's what my grandfather ultimately wanted me to learn—that for-profit businesses can do good too, that nonprofits should be run like for-profit businesses, and that maybe one of my missions in life is to get that word out. Of course writing a book about it is not actually doing it, but I like to think he would enjoy seeing me use my 20 years of experience to educate others so that more good can be accomplished.

I want you to walk away from this book with the feeling that you can do this. You can turn a dream you have into reality. You can make your reach in the world bigger by founding your own nonprofit. Not only can you do that, but you can do it well. You have the tools to use both the passion in your heart and the smarts in your brain to build a productive, well-run organization that marries the best ideas from the for-profit and nonprofit worlds to create something amazing. I can't wait to see where this journey takes you.

Resources

America's Small Business Development Centers:
  americassbdc.org

Applying for an Employer Identification Number—Internal
  Revenue Service: irs.gov (Search "Form SS-4")

Association of Fundraising Professionals: afpglobal.org
    Board Source: boardsource.org

The Chronicle of Philanthropy: philanthropy.org
    Charity Navigator: CharityNavigator.org

Consortium for Infant and Child Health: cinchcoalition.org
    Fiscal Sponsor Directory: fiscalsponsordirectory.org
    (National Network of Fiscal Sponsors:
    fiscalsponsors.org)

Grant Resources—The Foundation Center, by Candid:
  foundationcenter.org/candid.org

GuideStar by Candid: Guidestar.org

GrantSpace by Candid: grantspace.org

Incorporation in your state: Google "incorporating nonprofit
    corporation in _____ (insert state)" Internal Revenue
    Service: irs.gov

Job description (administrative associate) excerpt from
American Heart Association: https://www.indeed.
com viewjob?jk=1515301fc23c711a&tk=1djm-
mqgn7bs0h803&from=serp& vjs=3

Literacy Council of Northern Virginia: lcnv.org

The M.S. Hershey Foundation: mshersheyfoundation.org

National Council of Nonprofits:
https://www.councilofnonprofits.org

Needs Assessments Resources—
The Foundation Center, by Candid:
fconline.foundationcenter.org

Personnel Policy Information—U.S. Department of Labor:
dol.gov

*Real. Big. Love.: A Difference Maker's Guide to Gain
Greater Clarity, Energy, and Impact for Your Cause
and Life,* Lisa Wade

Robert's Rules of Order: robertsrules.org

SCORE (formerly the Service Corps of Retired Executives):
SCORE.org

United Way "Volunteer Agreement Form":
https://nonprofitdocuments.law.stanford.edu/
wp- content/uploads/
Volunteer-agreement-light-SLS-sample-06-27-17.pdf

VolunteerMatch: VolunteerMatch.org

Work for Good: workforgood.org

Acknowledgments

I had a heck of a lot of help bringing this book to fruition, from my coach and editor to my family and friends. I am so very grateful to everyone who supported me. First and foremost, thank you to my husband, Fred, who picked up the slack while I decided to go full-force into a new project, because when I decide to do something, I am all in. Secondly and just as important, a huge thank you to my beautiful daughters. I worked many hours on this, and getting it done would not have been possible without the few minutes of peace you gave me here and there to write. You are my inspiration to continue to make this world a better place. I hope I make you proud and give you the role model you need when you need it.

There are several people without whom I would not have undertaken this journey. A Real Big thank you and lots of Love goes to Lisa Wade, first a co-worker, then a coach, and always a friend. Without your love and support and belief in me, this project would never have even come to mind as a possibility. Your face makes me smile so big. Thank you also for the gift of introducing me to Maggie McReynolds of Un-Settling Books, who encouraged me from the moment we met. Maggie, your presence in itself is amazing, inspiring, and warm, and your ability to write and edit is brilliant. You helped me realize a dream and figure out that I am, indeed, a writer. Ready to do this again?

Thank you also to my college roommate, Jennifer, who suggested I start this endeavor because she had the confidence in my knowledge and ability that I didn't yet have. The world is only right when we're together. A huge sense of gratitude goes also to my other close supporters, including but not limited to the EC—you know who you are, and I could never have done this without your love, cheerleading, and excitement on my behalf. You love me the best all the time, and I love you. I want to thank those who contributed to this book, including Don Papson, Tammy Hiller, Michael Gingerich, and Tom Kaden. Your input was invaluable. I also want to express my gratitude to Patti Donnelly and Amy Paulson, two former bosses who were always and have remained friends. You both taught me more than you'll ever know. You showed me the best ways to make nonprofits flourish and make others feel special. Thank you for taking a chance on me and giving me incredible experiences that helped me grow.

This book would not have happened without the support of my parents as I began my nonprofit career and the loving generosity of my maternal grandparents and the inspiration of my grandfather, Richard A. Zimmerman. Despite his being gone for five years, his spirit is always with me, and I felt his guiding hand throughout this project. I know in my heart he is proud.

To my high school English teachers at Hershey High School who set me up with the best foundation for writing I could ever have had, thank you from the bottom of my heart. I went off to college more than prepared and into the real world ready to kick some grammatical ass. Thank you for reading all of my words, even when they weren't assignments but lifelines for someone to talk to. In memory of Edwin Knutsen and in honor of Alice Hamilton and Richard Bittinger, this book is as much as a nod to your teaching skills and ability to form relationships with students as it is about your enduring friendship and support. Thank you for believing in me.

Finally, a huge shout-out to baristas everywhere who memorized my order and kept my iced tea glass cold and full. I should have factored the cost of caffeine into the making of this book, or perhaps bought stock in Starbucks or Dunkin'.

About the Author

HILLARY B. MAROTTA

Hillary Marotta wears many hats, most of them align-
ing with her passion to help others. As a wife and mother
of two hilarious and energetic school-aged girls, her other
favorite roles include nonprofit specialist, Mental Health
First Aid Trainer, and musician. Hillary's 20-year career in
the nonprofit sector has taken her from education nonprofits to public health nonprofits, through teaching, managing
programs and projects, planning events, writing grants, and
obtaining funding. She recently served as a panelist, guest

speaker, and guest lecturer representing the nonprofit sector at the Women in Leadership Summit at Bucknell University in Lewisburg, Pennsylvania.

Hillary maintains involvement in many nonprofits including the Jubilee House Community-Center for Development in Central America (the Nicaraguan nonprofit that first touched her heart), the American Mental Wellness Association, and Grace United Methodist Church in Hummelstown, PA. She also serves on the Endowment Trust Board of the Hershey Library. From telling her own mental health story to listening to others and coordinating food bank volunteers and international shipments of medical supplies, Hillary is rarely at a loss for things to do. In her heart of hearts, she is a teacher through her book, her speaking engagements and work with nonprofits, and her desire to one day conduct a college level handbell choir. Hillary lives with her husband, two daughters, an adorable and personable goldendoodle and a less personable cat. She enjoys reading, writing, spending time with friends, and traveling. If she could live year-round in a tropical beach paradise, she would.

Thank You

Thank you for your desire to make a bigger impact and make the world a better place. And thank you for taking the time to read *Head and Heart: How to Run a Smart and Compassionate Nonprofit.* I am grateful for and appreciate the time you invested in this book, and I'd like to return the favor by supporting your work. I'd like to offer you the opportunity to connect with me one- on-one about your nonprofit idea via email at hillary@hillarymarotta.com. I'll also send you a free copy of my checklist for building a nonprofit so that you'll have a more bite-sized version of this book to refer to along the way.

In addition, if you feel like you, your organization, or your community could benefit from further discussion of the information in *Head and Heart,* I would love to help. Please feel free to find me at hillarymarotta.com and contact me at hillary@hillarymarotta.com to explore trainings, speaking engagements, and other ways of working together. I can also be found on Facebook @hillarymarottaauthor and at linkedin. com/in/hillarymarotta.

Endnotes

[1] Gregory Demetriou, Contributor, "Why New Nonprofits Fail.," HuffPost, April 23, 2017, Updated April 24, 2017, https://www.huffpost.com/entry/why-new-nonprofits-fail_b_58fc775ae4b0f02c3870eb5e, accessed May 23, 2019.

[2] "How many nonprofit organizations are there in the U.S.?" Candid. GRANTSPACE division, KNOWLEDGE BASE section,grantspace.org/resources/knowledge-base/number-of- nonprofits-in-the-u-s/accessed May 15, 2019.

[3] "Mission & Values: Red Cross Mission, Values, and Fundamental Principles," from the website for The American Red Cross, https://www.redcross.org/about-us/who-we-are/mission-and-values.html.

[4] "About" (page title), from the website for the Literacy Council of Northern Virginia, https://lcnv.org/about.

[5] "The M.S. Hershey Foundation (page title)," "Expanding the Foundation's Mission (paragraph title)," from the website Hershey Community Archives, September 7, 2018, https://hersheyarchives.org/encyclopedia/m-s-hershey-foundation/.

6 From the website for Someone To Tell It To, http://someonetotellitto.org.

7 "Groupthink," *Psychology Today,* https://www.psychologytoday.com/us/basics/groupthink, accessed May 10, 2019.

8 "Logic Model Development Guide," webpage, W. K. Kellogg Foundation, February 2, 2006, https://www.wkkf.org/resource-directory/resource/2006/02/wk-kellogg-foundation-logic-model-development-guide.

9 Resources for Job Creators, webpage, https://www.employer.gov/.

10 "Volunteering in U.S. Hits Record High; Worth $167 Billion" press release, Corporation for National & Community Service website, November 13, 2018, https://www.nationalservice.gov/newsroom/press-releases/2018/volunteering-us-hits-record- high-worth-167-billion, accessed May 5, 2019.

11 Thom Patterson, "Stats reveal how many Americans volunteer and where" webpage, Champions for Change series, Cable News Network (CNN) website, July 20, 2018, https://www.cnn.com/2018/07/19/us/volunteering-statistics-cfc/index.html, accessed July 16, 2019.

12 "Independent Sector Releases New value of Volunteer Time of $25.43 Per Hour" webpage, *Independent Sector* website, April 11, 2019, https://independentsector.org/news-post/new-value-volunteer-time-2019.

13 Mark Murphy, Contributor, "Neuroscience Explains Why You Need To Write Down Your Goals If You Actually Want To Achieve Them" webpage, *Forbes Magazine* website, April 16, 2018, https://www.forbes.com/sites/markmurphy/2018/04/15/neuroscience-explains-why-you-need-to-write-down-your-goals-if-you-actually-want-to-achieve-them/#540d22a77905, accessed May 27, 2019.

14 "Glossary of Nonprofit & Community Foundation Terms" webpage, *The Foundation for Enhancing Communities* (*TFEC*) website, (undated), https://www.tfec.org/glossary-of-nonprofit- community-foundation-terms.

15 Melanie Lockwood Herman, "The Garden of Risk Oversight: Positioning the Board to Cultivate Strategic Risk-Taking" webpage, *Nonprofit Risk Management Center* website, (undated), https://www.nonprofitrisk.org/resources/articles/garden-risk-oversight-positioning- board-cultivate-strategic-risk-taking/.

16 Lisa Wade Berry, *Real. Big. Love.: A Difference Maker's Guide to Gain Greater Clarity, Energy, and Impact for Your Cause and Life,* (2018).

17 Ann-Sophie Morrissette, "Five Myths that Perpetuate Burnout Across Nonprofits" webpage, *Stanford Social Innovation Review* website, October 31, 2016, https://ssir.org/articles/entry/five_myths_that_perpetuate_burnout_across_nonprofits.

Made in the USA
Middletown, DE
14 January 2023

22181745R00139